TEEN MANNERS
from Malls to Meals
to Messaging and Beyond

TEEN MANNERS

from Malls to Meals to Messaging and Beyond

BY CINDY POST SENNING, ED.D., AND PEGGY POST

Collins

An Imprint of HarperCollinsPublishers

Collins is an imprint of HarperCollins Publishers.

Teen Manners: From Malls to Meals to Messaging and Beyond
Text copyright © 2007 by Cindy Post Senning and Peggy Post
Illustrations copyright © 2007 by Sharon Watts

Library of Congress Cataloging-in-Publication Data
Senning, Cindy Post.
  Teen manners : from malls to meals to messaging and beyond / by Cindy
Post Senning and Peggy Post. — 1st ed.
    p. cm.
  ISBN 978-0-06-088198-6 (trade bdg.) — ISBN 978-0-06-088199-3 (lib. bdg.)
  1. Etiquette for children and teenagers. I. Post, Peggy, 1945– II. Title.
BJ1857.Y58S46 2007   2007010991
395.1'23—dc22   CIP
                                                             AC

Typography by Jeanne L. Hogle
1 2 3 4 5 6 7 8 9 10
❖
First Edition

We dedicate this book to our sons—Dan, Will, Casey, and Jeep—who shared with us the joys and challenges of their teen years.

ACKNOWLEDGMENTS

It is with deep appreciation that we acknowledge the following people for all their help with this book. We could not have done it without them:

Cheryl Family, whose knowledge about the teen years was essential throughout the writing and production of this book. Your contribution and suggestions about tone and voice were especially helpful. It has been a joy to work with you, and we look forward to our future efforts together.

Melanie Donovan and Greg Ferguson of HarperCollins, whose patience, support, and attention to detail kept us on track throughout the past year. An awesome editor is a gift and, Melanie, you are indeed awesome. Thank you!

Matt Bushlow, Elizabeth Howell, Katherine Cowles, and Peter Post, whose support, suggestions, and assistance were invaluable. You are all the best team we could hope for.

And all the teenagers out there who generously shared their thoughts and ideas throughout the project. After all, this is indeed your book!

Thank you all so very much!

CONTENTS

CHAPTER ONE

Why Etiquette?

In this chapter we'll cover:

1. Etiquette is really about relationships. It can help you start new relationships and build and strengthen those you already have.

2. Etiquette can shape the way you interact with people and create the mood for your day.

3. Etiquette can guide you in unfamiliar situations and tell you what you can expect from other people. It can make every new situation a little easier.

4. Etiquette is about choices. You can act in ways that are respectful, considerate, and honest, or not.

A FRENCH WORD FROM YESTERDAY FOR TODAY

In the seventeenth century King Louis XIV had a magnificent château with beautiful gardens and parks all around it. Often, when he hosted parties, people would walk all over the grass, pick the flowers, wade in the fountains, and leave litter behind. They didn't have formal gardens and parks at their own houses and didn't know how to behave. The head gardener went to the king in great distress and asked what he could do to keep things nicer. They decided to put up little signs all the over the place:

- KEEP ON THE PATHS
- ENJOY THE FLOWERS, BUT PLEASE DON'T PICK THEM
- STAY OUT OF THE FOUNTAINS
- PLEASE DON'T LITTER

The French word for "little sign" or "ticket" is *etiquette*. All these years later, etiquette still is simply a collection of "little signs" to guide us in unfamiliar situations. That guidance helps us get along better with others and feel more comfortable everywhere.

WHAT IS ETIQUETTE?

When asked this question, people often respond:
- Saying please
- Manners

- Which fork you use
- Taking off your hat
- Thank-you notes
- Respect
- Caring for others

All of them are right. Some talk about specific manners, and some talk about principles that help us get along. Etiquette is actually a combination of both.

No matter what they think etiquette is, most people agree that it is important.

WHAT ETIQUETTE IS NOT

- A little pinkie stuck up in the air as you drink your tea
- A limp-fish handshake
- An officious, superior attitude toward others
- A bow tie and white gloves
- Old-fashioned and only for some people

A FORMULA FOR SUCCESS

Etiquette = Manners + Principles

MANNERS MATTER

Manners tell you what to do in a myriad of situations. Are you going to a wedding and wondering what's expected? There are manners that will help you out. Are you going to your sister's concert and trying to decide what to wear? There are manners to guide your decision. Are you unsure how to reply to a party invitation? There are manners to help you respond, whether or not you can go. Sometimes manners tell you what to do in specific situations; sometimes they tell you what you can expect others to do.

PRINCIPLES MATTER MORE

So how do manners come into being? Who decides and how? That's where the principles come in. All manners are rooted in just three principles:

1. Respect: caring for and understanding others just as they are—whether they look different, come from different cultures, or have different beliefs. It is important to show respect for everyone with all his or her differences and similarities. And you look to others to show respect for you.

2. Consideration: thinking about how your actions will affect others around you.

3. Honesty: more than just not telling lies. If the truth might be hurtful, it means finding the most positive

FINDING THE POSITIVE TRUTH

Your grandmother has cooked all day to make a special dinner. She notices you haven't eaten the spinach and asks you, "What's the matter? Don't you like the spinach?"

You don't say, "Thanks, Grandmother, but I'm full" (a lie that will become painfully obvious if you eat a huge piece of cake for dessert).

Instead, you find the positive: "You know, Grandmother, spinach has never been my favorite, but this chicken is the best I ever had."

You won't need to worry that she'll expect you to eat a lot of spinach again. And it had better be an honest statement about the chicken because she will be sure to cook it for you!

way you can to tell it... or sometimes keeping silent.

These principles are timeless and universal. Manners, the ways that people apply the principles of etiquette, change over time and from culture to culture, but the principles do not. It is respectful to greet someone when you meet, but the specifics of the greeting may be different. In some cultures you shake hands, in some you bow, but in all cultures the respectful thing to do is to greet the people you meet.

You can trace every manner in this book

back to one of the principles. When society changes and new behaviors emerge (cell phone use, for instance), new manners develop too. For example, using a cell phone inconsiderately by talking really loudly on the phone at the movies disturbs other people. So the movie management might post a NO CELL PHONES sign. Soon people learn that loud talking in movie theaters is unacceptable. Over time those behaviors that show consideration and respect become the accepted norm, and new manners emerge.

Sometimes manners become obsolete. For example, it used to be accepted manners that the girl never called the boy for a date. Today girls often call boys and ask them out.

No matter what the situation is or where you find yourself, if you don't know the manners, all you need do is choose to act in a respectful, considerate, and honest way, and you'll do well. Whether or not you know the specific manners, you can act in a way that makes those around you feel good. Knowing the manners just makes it a bit easier. And while being considerate, respectful, or honest sometimes seems to benefit just the other person, it can make you a better person.

THE ULTIMATE BENEFIT

Etiquette is all about relationships. When you meet someone and make your first impression, you set that relationship off in one direction. Changing direction is doable but difficult. Why not start out on the right path to begin with? Acting toward that person with respect and consideration—using good manners—will set things up in the best way possible.

Once the relationship is established, you can choose to build and strengthen it or not. How does it feel when a friend greets you warmly as if he is truly glad to see you? It's not rocket science. It really is that easy. All it takes is intention. Make using good manners a habit. Make the principles of etiquette the basis for how you act. If you do, you'll have the tools you need to begin, build, and strengthen all your relationships with friends and family. In addition, by choosing to use good etiquette, you'll develop a sense of self-respect and self-confidence that will make you a better friend and family member.

CHAPTER TWO

Build and Strengthen EVERY Relationship

In this chapter we'll cover:
   1. How what you say matters and other important reminders about language
   2. How what you do matters
   3. How your image matters

You have a crazy day ahead of you: You're meeting with your history teacher about the first draft of your major term paper, you and your girlfriend are meeting for lunch, and you need to ask your mom for a ride after school to your first job interview. You think you should wear a jacket and tie to the job interview, but your girlfriend will think you look weird and are going against who you really are. You've had an argument with your mom and are worried she won't give you the ride. Also, you don't feel prepared for the conference with your teacher. In ten short hours you're dealing with at least four different relationships, all of which are really important to you.

YOUR LANGUAGE: HOW WHAT YOU SAY MATTERS

It's All About Talk

What you say and how you say it form the foundation for every one of your relationships, whether it's with your friends, your teachers, or your family. You may be incredibly talkative and spend hours in conversation with all sorts of people. You may be the quiet type and ground your social interactions in what you do together rather than how much you say. Whichever is your style, whether you're talking to your grandparents or your best friend, the words you choose and the way you use them will affect how well you get along with other people.

Is there still magic in those magic words you learned when you were just two years old?

Please makes things happen more smoothly.

Your good friend says, "*Let me have your cell phone; I need to call Carla.*"

OR

Your good friend says, "*Could I please use your cell phone?*

I left mine at home today, and I need to call Carla."

In either case, your friend uses your cell phone to call Carla, and the day goes on.

But *please* has changed a demand into a request. Making a request of someone rather than demanding something really conveys how you feel about that person. If you demand, you may get what you want (or you may not), but your relationship suffers—even if just a small amount. If you request, you may get what you want (or you may not), but nobody is left feeling bad.

Thank you shows appreciation. It makes the person you're thanking feel good.

You find an iPod under the bench in a hallway at school. It has a name on it, B. Andrews. You take the time to go to the office, find out B. Andrews's homeroom, and take it to her the next morning. She sort of grabs it and says, *"Where'd you find it? I knew it would turn up sometime."*

OR

She tells you, *"Phew! Thanks a lot . . . I couldn't remember where I left it. I really appreciate your taking the time to track me down!"*

When there is a reason for thanks, someone has usually done something for you. Sometimes it has taken time and thought, extra effort, or money. By showing your appreciation, you acknowledge that. The person you thank is likely to feel good and will be much more likely to repeat the effort.

You're welcome acknowledges *thanks*. Acknowledging another person tells her you understood and appreciated what she said or did.

It's not much, but what an easy way to let you know that she heard your thanks. Without it, she might wonder if you were really sort of irritated at being spoken to or something.

Your friend has just given you a ride. You say, "*Thanks. You've just saved me a long walk.*" Your friend just drives on.

OR

Your friend says, "*You're welcome. Anytime!*"

Excuse me acknowledges a breach of good manners of some sort and helps smooth the way.

You're having lunch with three of your good friends. One of them is telling about the crazy thing that happened over the weekend. You open your mouth to comment and instead of words you come out with a wicked burp! You say nothing and hope no one noticed.

OR

You can say, "*Oh, no! Excuse me.*" Everyone laughs, and the conversation continues.

Whether it's a burp, someone bumping into someone, an emergency, or a break into someone's conversation, *excuse me* can take out the irritation that is likely to follow.

WHERE'S THE MAGIC?

Someone has bumped into you. He says:

WORDS	TONE	WHAT HE'S REALLY SAYING
Excuse me.	Oh, excuse me.	I didn't see you there! Sorry.
Excuse me.	Well, excu-use me.	What the heck were you doing in my way anyhow?

They're the same words; there is no magic in them.
The "magic" is in the way they're said.

##@!! or Delete Expletive

Multiple choice

You drop a can of tomatoes on your toe. It hurts! You say:

1. OW-W-W!

2. *##*@!!

3. Oy, that hurts!

If you are in the family life education classroom with your teacher right there, you might choose 1 or 3.

If you are with your two good friends, you might use 1, 2, or 3.

If you are with your mother, it is likely to depend on what she would say in the same situation.

The actual words you use won't fix your toe. It's bad enough that you've dropped the can on your foot and it hurts. Why should you compound it by offending your teacher or your mother? It's clear that the words may not seem offensive to you, but they may be to some of the people in your life. In the long run it's your choice; the key thing is to consider the effect you may have on someone important to you.

SECRETS, RUMORS, GOSSIP: WHEN WHAT YOU *DON'T* SAY MATTERS MOST

One of the benefits to having a good relationship is that you can talk something through and trust that your friend will keep it confidential. One of the most painful events in a relationship is the betrayal of a confidence. It may be in the form of a secret revealed, a rumor started, or gossip continued. Trust is a valuable commodity. Once trust is lost, a relationship is diminished, and it takes ages to rebuild—all because someone said something that shouldn't have been said. Keep this in mind the next time you're about to share someone else's secret.

It takes two . . .

Languages, that is: body and spoken.

Picture this: Marie's parents have been divorced for three years. She sees her father only every other weekend. One weekend her father tells her he has something important to talk about. Marie loves her dad but really was hoping to be with her

friends that morning. However, she
agrees to spend time with him. He
begins to tell her about the little
house that he is hoping to buy. It
will be closer to her, and they will
be able to see each other more
often. Marie nods and says all the

"correct" things, but she is slouching in her
chair, thumbing through a magazine, and repeatedly glancing at
the clock. Her dad quickly ends the conversation and offers to
take her to her friend's. "No, no," she says, "tell me about the
house. What's wrong?"

Marie didn't realize that while her words were good, she
was nonetheless sending a clear message that she was bored.
Her body language said it all. Fortunately she recognized
that something had gone flat and made the effort to show
her father she cared about what he had to say. She
acknowledged a problem, sat up, smiled, and fully engaged

in the conversation. But if she hadn't,
her body language, which was
contradicting her verbal language,
would have resulted in a
miscommunication.

YOUR ACTIONS: HOW WHAT YOU DO MATTERS

Introductions

Introducing people is one of the most important etiquette skills you can learn. Many people think it is complicated and confusing, so they don't do it and leave people in the awkward position of not knowing whom they are talking to. Introductions are not that difficult. Whether you are introducing yourself, introducing two people you know who have never met each other, or being introduced to someone, the goal of the introduction is for all involved to know who is who.

Self-introductions

First impressions can make or break you. A good introduction can make the difference between a good first impression and a bad one. There are five basic steps to a good self-introduction.

1. If you're seated, stand up. This puts people at equal eye level with no one looking down on anyone. If you're entering the room, approach the other person with confidence.

2. Look the other person in the eye and *smile*. You're trying to make a good first impression here, and a good smile always helps.

3. Shake hands—a gesture of friendship.

4. Introduce yourself: "Hi, I'm Jackie. I just joined the team." The other person should respond by shaking your hand and telling you her name: "Hi, Jackie, I'm Susie. Glad to meet you. Have you played soccer on a team somewhere else?"

5. Say the person's name. This reinforces her name in your head and gives her the opportunity to correct it right then if you heard it wrong. "Glad to meet you too, Susie. No, this is my first time trying out."

The steps are easy, as with every skill, you get better if you practice. Go over the steps with someone you know. Then, when you are faced with introducing yourself to a stranger, it will go more smoothly, and you can focus on the person rather than how you are doing with the introduction. You will also appear more confident because you most likely are.

Introducing one person to another

Sometimes people skip doing introductions because they worry about making a mistake. The following tips will help you with the trickiest parts of any introduction.

Introduce the younger person to the older person. The trick here is to say the older person's name first:

"Mr. Hernandez, this is my friend Maria."

"Grandmother, I want you to meet my teacher Mrs. Kim."

If it is not clear who is older, then it doesn't make much difference as long as you do the introduction.

Pronounce names clearly. Use an adult's title and last name. *"Dad, this is my coach, Miss Walinski."* When you know it, include a little description that helps people understand the connections. "*Dad, this is my coach, Miss Walinski. She's the one I told you about who taught me to improve my foul shots.*" This also gives people a little background so they can start up conversations on their own, independent of you.

Make the introduction even if you've forgotten the person's name. Just introduce yourself first to the person whose name you forgot. "*I'm sorry. I know we've met, but I don't remember your name. I'm Jose Garcia, and this is my friend Ali Tessa.*"

When you are being introduced to someone, follow the same steps you use in self-introductions:

- ◉ Stand, or if you're already standing, turn to face him.
- ◉ Look him in the eye and smile.
- ◉ Shake hands.
- ◉ Respond with something simple and straightforward like "It's good to meet you, Mr. O'Brien."

If you want to make a good impression on this first meeting, you'll want to avoid . . .

- ◉ Looking at the ground or away when you are being introduced to someone
- ◉ Refusing to shake a hand extended in greeting

◉ Crunching someone's hand in a bone-crushing grip or offering your hand as if it's a wet dishrag

A Hand Extended in Friendship

That's what a handshake is. In medieval times, when your face was covered by a metal mask and helmet, the person you were meeting didn't know if you were friend or foe. You extended your right hand so the other person could see there was no sword or other weapon in it. The person you were meeting returned the gesture, showed an empty hand, and shook hands, completing a greeting that said "friend."

A HANDSHAKE: THE BASICS

◆ Extend your right hand, thumb up, palm flat.

◆ Grasp the other person's hand firmly palm to palm.

◆ Pump your hand two or three times.

◆ Release.

Practice this a few times with friends or family. Try different pressures and hanging on for fifteen pumps or just one. You'll quickly discover what's comfortable for you and the other person. It's much easier to get it right with someone you know than to try it out for the first time with a stranger.

Introduction Dilemmas

What do you do when . . . ?

@ **You are watching the NBA final playoff game.** The score is tied, there is one minute left, and your grandmother arrives for a visit. You haven't seen her for six months.

Stand up; welcome your grandmother with a big hug, and ask her if she minds if you finish watching the game. You could even invite her to watch with you; she might enjoy it too.

@ **You are in the inside seat of a booth in a restaurant with your parents.** A friend from school comes into the restaurant with his parents. When he sees you, he comes over to introduce them. You can't really stand up.

You make the effort as if to stand, reach over the table to shake hands, and greet your friend and his parents. Then introduce your parents to your friend and his parents. *"Hi, Mr. and Mrs. James. It's good to meet you. Mom and Dad, this is my friend Pat James and his parents."*

@ **You're sitting in the food court at the mall.** You've just taken a mouthful of pizza when your friend comes by and introduces his cousin, who is visiting.

Keep your mouth closed and point to it, chew and swallow as quickly as you safely can, and then say, *"Hi, Kamal, nice to meet you!"* Stand up too if you're able to get up from the table easily.

GREETINGS

Picture this: Jake has had a bad start to his day. His alarm didn't go off, he missed his breakfast, he left his homework on the kitchen table, he saw his girlfriend flirting with the new guy in their class, and it's only eight in the morning. BUT he's sitting at his desk waiting for class to start, and his good buddy Jill walks in the room, gives him a huge smile, and says, *"Hey, hi!"* Jake immediately feels just a little bit better.

The greeting sets the tone. A cheerful, friendly greeting leaves people feeling good; no greeting leaves people wondering; a sullen greeting may leave people feeling bad. It's really amazing. Something as simple as how you say hi can affect someone's day—even one that has started as badly as Jake's. It also affects the day of the person who makes the greeting. It's hard to make a smile without feeling just a little bit better. Try it.

Who goes first? It really doesn't matter. The important thing is that two people greet each other.

A FEW COMMON COURTESIES

On Time

Being on time is one of the easiest ways to show respect and consideration for the people you are with. On the flip side, being late shows both disrespect and inconsideration for those you are meeting. When you're late, you are saying,

"I think my time is more important than yours" or "I'm not really very organized." Definitely not good messages to send.

If you're not early, you're *late*!

Timeliness is mostly a mind-set. People who are always on time have developed a habit of planning. They know that "If you're not early, you're late!" There is only an instant that represents "on time." All other instants are either early or late.

People who are chronically late often operate on the premise that if they are early, they will lose that time, and they already don't have enough time. The trick is to plan for those ten minutes so they are not "wasted." You could . . .

- Review your notes for the meeting
- Make a restroom stop and freshen up
- Carry a small book or magazine to read
- Meditate
- Check messages
- Send a quick text message

After You

You and your friends are approaching the mall entrance. You get to the door first. You have a choice: Go straight on through, or pull the door open and gesture to your friends "you first." If there is someone with several packages coming out the door, a young mother with a stroller, or a person in a wheelchair or with a cane, hold the door for her. It's so easy to

make someone's day; sometimes all it takes is holding a door. And you might hear, "What a nice young person," or just, "Thank you." Either feels good and can make your day too.

LIVING WITH OTHERS

Whether you live in an apartment or a house, share a room with a sibling, have your own room, go to boarding school and have a roommate, or go to camp and share a cabin with four others, some spaces are private and some are shared. It is important to work out the ground rules for both those areas and then to stick to them wherever you are.

Private Spaces

A closed door is a request for privacy. Knock and wait to be asked in before entering.

Private space includes the furniture: bureaus, bedside tables, beds, bunks, and drawers.

Diaries, journals, and letters are private. They may never be opened or read without the owner's permission.

Phone calls are private, and listening in is an invasion of privacy.

Keep your things in your own personal area.

Borrowing: The Bottom Line

Ask before using anything that belongs to someone else: clothes, cell phone, electronic games, iPod, camera, books, car, bike, sports equipment, etc. Remember the golden rule? Just think how you would feel if someone used your things without asking. Then you'll know whether or not you need to ask.

The etiquette about borrowing is simple: If you break it or use it up, you replace it.

So the bottom line is: If you can't pay to replace it, don't borrow it!

Q & A

Question: You are in a crowded elevator or train, and someone at the back wants to get out. What should you do?

Answer: If you are near the open-door button, push it so that the person is able to exit. If you are in front of the person who wants to exit, step out, let him get out, and step back in.

Shared Spaces

The living room, the kitchen, and the bathroom all have one thing in common. They are shared spaces. Living with another person does require compromise: You have to negotiate phone, computer, TV, and stereo use; you also need to know who cleans what and establish a neatness standard. As with private spaces, the important thing is to work out the ground rules and then stick to them.

Living/family room

◎ Clean up after yourself.

◎ Take care not to monopolize the space and the things in the space; remember it is shared.

◎ Casual or formal? Stick to the ground rules you've established.

Kitchen

◎ Clean up after yourself.

◎ Check before eating something that might be intended for a special meal.

◎ If you eat the last of everyone's favorite food, add it to the shopping list or replace it.

Bathroom

◎ Clean up after yourself.

◎ Hang wet towels up to dry.

◎ Put dirty clothes in the hamper.

◎ Replace the empty toilet paper roll.

◎ Take care not to hog the bathroom.

◎ Respect closed doors.

Shared spaces have to be cleaned; trash has to be picked up and taken out; recyclables have to be sorted and put out; pets and plants have to be tended; laundry has to be washed, dried, folded, and put away. There are a myriad of chores associated with living together. The most common and reasonable courtesy that will make life just a little bit better for all involved is to share those chores. Rather than assume someone else will take care of it, either just do it or plan how you will divide the chores. Without a strategy, resentments often develop as one person in the group begins to think that the others aren't pulling their weight. You choose: resentment or cooperation.

SOCIAL CLEANING: WHO KNEW?

Consider a cleaning schedule and make it fun. Tuesday night is cleaning night. Everyone picks out his favorite music and special snacks and drinks, and let the work begin. By making it more social, you won't think it's a downer. If some chores are nastier than others, create a rotation so everyone shares in the tough jobs.

WHAT TO WEAR?

What Image Do You Want? What Image Do You Have?

Your appearance is a unique opportunity to tell the world about yourself.

Picture this: You walk into a room. There are four people there whom you don't know. Before anyone has even said a word, those four people have made an impression on you.

What is the image you present? After all, you only get one chance to make a first impression on others, and that first impression may make a big difference. At an interview for a job or school admission you might want to create an image that shows you are competent, organized, and mature. At a party you might want to create an image that shows you are creative, have a sense of fun, and fit in with the group. At school you might want to show your fashion sense while abiding by the dress code. Regardless of the image you want to project, there are some questions you can ask yourself before you go out to any event. The following four questions can be answered with a yes or no. You choose.

1. Are your clothes clean?

2. Are your clothes torn, mismatched, stained, or wrinkled?

3. Do your clothes fit?

4. Are you dressed appropriately?

Beyond the Clothes

Personal hygiene

What's the point of putting on clean clothes over a dirty body? You need to be clean too. This means:

- Brushing your teeth
- Showering regularly
- Using deodorant if necessary

Hairstyles

Your hair sends the same message as your clothes. Are you an athlete, a drama major, a singer in a rock band, a scientist? Does your hairstyle reflect your image? Is it one that takes time to keep up? Does your hairstyle help or get in the way of what you want to do? Whether you have dreads, a shaved head, a ponytail, bangs, multicolors, straight hair, or a mass of curls, there is one word that cannot be overlooked and applies to all: CLEAN! Nothing will turn people off more quickly than a head of greasy, smelly, dirty hair.

It is also important to consider the situation. If you have long hair and are going to a party, you may wear it flying free. When you go in for the job or college interview, you may choose to braid it or pull it back. The key is to give your hair some thought. Not only does one style not fit everyone, but everyone may have more than one style. You need to feel comfortable.

Tattoos and body piercing

One of the joys of clothing and hair is that you can experiment with different looks. With tattoos and body piercing—not so.

Picture this: Jared is sixteen and in love. He knows Marie is the girl for him. He makes his way to the local tattoo shop and has *Marie* tattooed in dark red across the knuckles of his right hand. Three months later Marie leaves him for another guy. Maybe it's not *Marie*. Maybe he has a dragon winding its way up his arm or a devil on his neck and then wants to join a gospel group. The point is tattoos are permanent. They can be removed only with considerable pain and expense. So be sure it's something you can live with forever before getting inked. Unless, of course, you opt for a henna tattoo that wears off in time.

Body piercing is less permanent, but there is a different issue to consider. Body piercing seems to elicit a negative reaction from those who don't understand its appeal. At your grandmother's, your interview, in class, or at your job you might want to consider using an understated ring or stud that will not overwhelm. There might even be times you would want to take the stud out.

Too much or too little

Makeup and perfume or aftershave are worn to enhance your image. There is nothing more appealing than a gentle hint of that special scent. Subtlety is the key. In fact we often associate a particular scent with a special event or person.

On the other hand, have you ever been stuck in a closed room with someone drowning in perfume or aftershave? Some people actually feel physically sick from an overpowering scent.

Consider carefully the lasting impression you want to leave, and remember that there is such a thing as too much of a good thing.

Issues about your image may arise between you and your parents, your teachers, and your coaches as you begin making choices for yourself. You will have to decide which are the ones that are most important to you. If you can show maturity in decisions about your image, you will also show maturity about your

ability to make other decisions. Only you can decide which choices will best reflect who you are. This goes deeper than your outward look; it also reflects who you are becoming inside.

CHAPTER THREE

Keeping in Touch

In this chapter we'll cover:
> **1.** The manners for modern communications tools, including cell phones, e-mail, IMing, and more
> **2.** What to do when those around you forget their mobile manners
> **3.** Telephone manners at home

You're talking on the phone to your mom to let her know you're home, e-mailing a friend about the day's gossip, and—oh, wait—here comes an IM from your classmate asking about tonight's homework. You're totally connected. Life is good!

But you just told your mom about Brad kissing Marci after Spanish and your classmate that you're home from school and the meat loaf for dinner is in the oven. Whoops!

Even if you can multitask like no one else, you can still get your wires crossed.

E-MAIL AND ONLINE MANNERS

To go along with recent technological inventions, new manners have been invented. Portable gadgets can be great conveniences, but they can also annoy people around us. In general, any time your use of a technodevice is going to disturb other people, either turn it off or move to a place where it won't be a problem.

Here are some more specific "new" manners to help you: Don't use an electronic device while you are involved in another activity. Don't play with your Game Boy when you're at your brother's band concert. Turn off your cell phone before you go into church. Follow any rules posted wherever you are: school, restaurant, movies, place of worship, or concert hall.

E-mail

E-mail makes communicating easier than ever. You can write a letter to your friend—no stamp necessary—and have it delivered instantly. Websites and desktop publishing programs offer e-postcards and e-greeting cards for all occasions as well. Just as with other types of communication, a whole set of manners has evolved to help us all be considerate and respectful as e-mail races back and forth across the Internet.

Make Sure You . . .

◉ Check over what you've written before clicking "send." Sending e-mail is like dropping a letter in the mail slot: You can't get it back.

◉ Write only what you're willing to have all the world see. It's very easy for someone to forward your note or cut and paste it into a message of his own.

◉ Respect others' privacy. Don't forward a message someone has sent you in confidence.

◉ Use the subject line. This lets e-mail recipients know that your message isn't spam.

◉ Use "reply all" with care. You may not really want everybody on the list to see your reply.

◉ Respond as promptly as possible. Let the sender know you got her message, and if you don't have time at the moment, you'll write more later.

Take Care Not to . . .

◉ Open strange e-mail. If it is not from an address you know, delete it immediately.

◉ WRITE IN CAPS. This is considered

Q & A

Question: My friend is always sending me annoying chain e-mails and weird jokes. How can I get her to stop?

Answer: If you're the victim of "friend spam" clogging up your in-box and wasting your time, simply delete it. If after a while your friend receives no response or comment from you, she may stop sending them. Or you can speak up and ask her to stop—politely and honestly: "Tara, I like hearing from you, but please stop sending me e-mail jokes. I'm too busy to read them all. Thanks!"

shouting, and it's hard to read.

◉ Send attachments unless you know the recipient has the software to open them.

◉ Write when you are upset. If you are mad about something, wait until you've calmed down before writing about it. That way you won't have anything to regret.

The guidelines you would use to write a letter also apply to e-mail correspondence: Greet the person, think about the content, check spelling and grammar, and use an appropriate closing. Just because e-mail is quick and easy to use, there is no need to be lazy about regular letter-writing manners. It shows a lack of respect you may not intend.

The Top Five Ways to Misuse Your E-mail

1. Spreading hurtful gossip or untrue stories
2. Avoiding face-to-face conversations

3. Going into gruesome personal detail about yourself or someone else

4. Spamming

5. Criticizing another person

Message Board Manners

Message boards and chat rooms let people share ideas across the country and the world. But it's no different from any other time you get together with friends. There are ways to make it a better experience for everyone. Here are eight tips for safe, fun visits to chat rooms and message boards:

1. Never, ever for any reason share personal information, such as your real name, address, phone number, age, and sex. If anyone in the chat room asks you for this information, just log off.

2. If the chat room is specific for a certain topic, talk only about that topic, not about something else.

3. Keep your questions and answers short.

4. Use appropriate language. Bad language is bad manners in any public forum. The fact that no one knows you is no excuse.

5. Be nice. The old expression "You catch more flies with honey than with vinegar" applies to chat rooms and message boards. If someone is being mean and nasty to you, don't be mean and nasty back; just log off.

6. Don't use ALL CAPS! It's rude.

7. Read carefully. Just as in a face-to-face conversation, you may learn something if you pay attention to what other people are writing.

8. Let the others in the chat room know when you arrive and when you leave. It is good manners to say hello and good-bye in any setting.

Remember, if you are bullied or mistreated in any way, you have no social obligation to stay. Online time is meant to be a good time. If it's not, simply move on. Follow your instincts. If something feels strange, it probably is, and you should end the session. It is your choice to log on and your choice to log off. Make the one that's right for you.

SOCIAL NETWORKING 101

Sites such as MySpace, Friendster, and Facebook are a great way to connect with friends—new and old. Here are a few tips that can help you be more successful with your site.

◉ Your web page can be viewed by anyone, not just your friends. Employers, college admissions officers, and family members may also visit your page. So think twice about what you post (or allow others to post).

◉ If you want to post photos of others, ask their permission first.

◉ Don't accept friend requests from people you don't know.

◉ It's all right to ask others to remove from their

page a photo or comment about you that you
don't like.

⊚ If for any reason you don't like a comment or
image left on your page by someone else, it's okay
to delete it.

⊚ It's never okay or cool to contribute to or
visit pages that make fun of a classmate or
acquaintance.

FAMILY AND FRIENDS

Unless you are alone in your room using a computer
game on your own line, your use of the new technology will
have an effect on someone else. Even if you can't see your
mother while she is in the kitchen, be considerate of her.
Before you tie up the line with an extended IMing session
with your friends, be sure she doesn't need the phone. If
the cordless phone is under the covers in your bedroom,
no one else in the family can use it, and the batteries will
probably run out. If your friend is visiting and you spend the
whole time on your handheld computer game, she may not
come back.

Technomanners haven't all been set. For example, what's
up with camera phones in locker rooms? Some new
technology that you haven't even thought of will be in your
home tomorrow. There may not be manners to guide you in
its use. When that's the case, it will be up to you to decide what

to do. If you base your decisions on respect, consideration, and honesty, they will always be good ones.

Telephone Manners

Are you lucky enough to have a separate computer line or a cell phone? Or is your family sharing one home phone line? Are you jockeying for access with a brother or sister? The following phone manners basics can give you an advantage in getting access to, and time on, that phone. They will also make those shorter times you are on all the more productive.

Answer the phone with a nice greeting

When you make a call, say hello and identify yourself. Score points by acknowledging the person who answers if you know her: *"Hello, Mrs. Able, this is Jeremy. May I please talk to Alex?"*

Why? Think about it. What sounds better, the above greeting or a curt *"Is Alex home?"*

It's all in the tone. Your hello can sound warm and friendly or nasty and sullen; the choice is yours. If the call is for someone else, keep it simple: *"Just a minute, I'll get her."* Or if you know the caller, *"Oh, hi, Mrs. Blake. Hold on, I'll get her."* Place the phone down gently so it doesn't go clunk in her ear. Instead of standing there and screaming, *"Dad, it's for you!!!!!"* go get the person it's for. If you know who the caller is, say so: *"Mom, it's Mrs. Blake."*

If the person being called isn't there, offer to take a message: *"Jackson isn't here right now; may I take a message?"* When you take a message, write down the name of the caller, his phone number, and the time and date of the call. If your family doesn't have a place where you leave messages for one another, establish one. That way you won't have to worry about messages getting lost or overlooked. If you listen to a voice mail or answering machine message that's for someone else, be sure to tell that person about it.

SO WHAT WOULD YOU DO?

Your dad's coworker called, and you forgot to give him the message. You would . . .

1. Just pretend it never happened.
2. Tell Dad ASAP and apologize.
3. Blame it on your sister.

Okay, the correct answer is 2: Let your dad know about the call as soon as you remember and apologize. Then it's over. If Dad makes the same mistake and 'fesses up, be sure to accept his apology too. If nothing else, you'll be setting a good example for your parents to follow!

Are there rules in your family about phone use? You're not alone. Many families establish rules about phones and phone use. There's a lot to consider:

◉ How long is it okay to talk? If you don't have call-waiting or caller ID, the considerate thing is to limit calls to whatever time your family agrees is reasonable.

🌀 What times are okay for calling? A good guide is no earlier than nine in the morning and no later than nine at night. You might call before or after those times if you know a friend's family doesn't mind.

🌀 Is it okay to make long-distance calls? It depends what kind of phone plan your family has. Certain long-distance calls could rack up considerable phone bills! Make sure you're clear on what's okay and what's not.

There's no reason why you can't be included in the discussion when it comes to setting household phone rules. If your goal is more liberal phone use, try a constructive approach; don't just compare what your friend's family does with your parent's "archaic" methods. Instead, put together a thoughtful plan that includes a reasonable length of time for phone use. If your plan addresses the issues you know are important to others in the family, it is more likely to be accepted. Be prepared to compromise. You might not get everything you want, but you'll be ahead of where you are now.

Be Safe!

Don't give your name when answering the phone. If it's a wrong number, just say so without giving out your number. If a stranger calls, don't let him know if you are home alone. If someone asks for a parent, just say, "She can't come to the phone right now. May I take a message?" If a caller gets obnoxious or starts to say strange things, just hang up. Tell your parents about the call. If you have an answering machine or caller ID, you can use it to screen calls when you're home alone.

CALLER ID

Question: I know who is calling. Can't I just pick up the phone and say, "Hi, Joe"?

Answer: If it is someone you speak to frequently or you know that a particular person calls at that time, you can say hi in a way that indicates you know who it is. Otherwise you are better off just to say hello. The name of the person who owns the phone number is indicated on the caller ID, but you don't know for sure it's that person. Someone else could be using that phone, and then you have the awkwardness associated with the person saying, "No, it's Marika. I'm just using Joe's phone."

Caller ID is an amazing tool. It is helpful to know who is actually interrupting what you are doing, and it gives control to you. You can choose whether or not you want to answer the phone. It gives you the option of knowing the person is trying to reach you and calling her back at a time that is more convenient for you.

Call-waiting: Helpful or a Pain in the Neck?

A manners basic that you probably learned when you were four is "Don't interrupt." So you're on the phone with a friend and call-waiting beeps. That's an interruption, isn't it?

What do you do?

🌀 If the signal can be heard by both of you, say, "There's call-waiting. I just need to check who it is. Hold on a sec. I'll be right back." If your friend can't hear the beep, wait until he ends his sentence and then interrupt.

🌀 If the call is for you, say you're on the line and you'll call right back. Go back to your first friend, finish the conversation, and call your other friend back soon.

🌀 If the call is for your mother, ask the person to hold while you get her. Then go back to your friend, tell him there is a call for your mother and you'll call him back, and then get your mother so she can take her call. Why? It's a way to show respect, and your mom will appreciate your consideration. She may even do the same for you the next time your friend beeps in while she's on the phone.

CELL PHONES

Cell Phone Anarchy

Once upon a time, not too long ago, there were no cell phones. Being able to call or get calls no matter where you were was the stuff of science fiction. So there were no manners for a phone you could use anywhere. With no rules to guide them, people just used this new tool anywhere and any way they saw fit. Slowly, as more people got cell phones, it became clear that there were some really inconsiderate behaviors going on. Movie theaters, churches, and restaurants began putting up signs asking people to turn off their ringers. In schools, rules limiting or banning cell phone use were laid down. In places where one person's use of a cell phone would affect the others sharing that space, some general manners evolved.

The Top Five Cell Phone Turnoffs

1. Talking too loudly. Whenever you make a call in public, speak as quietly as you can. Don't shout into your phone while walking outdoors. Talking loudly forces everyone around you to listen in, whether he wants to or not.

2. Leaving the ringer on in quiet places. Theaters, places of worship, and funerals should always be cell phone–free zones, as should most enclosed spaces where you can't maintain a ten-foot distance from other people. The vibrator mode signals incoming calls without disturbing others for anyone who must remain on call. If someone doesn't absolutely need to be able to reach you, turn the phone off.

3. Ignoring those you're with. The people you're with

come first. If you make or take calls when you're in the middle of a face-to-face conversation, you're making whoever you're with feel second best.

4. Making repeated calls. Keep calls to a minimum on public transportation, in line at the bank or movies, and in busy areas like airports. Placing one call after another (especially just to pass the time) eventually exasperates even the most understanding captive listener. Barring an emergency, limit your calls, or move to a more private spot.

5. Using inappropriate language. Some cell phone users (including otherwise well-spoken people) feel free to use obscenities in public. There's no reason to risk offending those around you. A good rule of thumb is to skip the foul language whenever you are in public.

Q & A

Question: I was in the bathroom at a restaurant, and the woman in the stall next to me was using her cell phone. Is no place sacred? Can anything be done in a situation like this?

Answer: Who wants to listen to another person's phone conversation in the bathroom? The bathroom is supposed to be a private space even if it's a public restroom. When someone comes in to make a call, that person is invading your privacy by forcing you to listen in. (Not to mention that she's hogging the stall!) Mobile users, listen up: When you'd like to make a call, take it outside.

IM EVOLUTION

Instant messaging is an evolving form of communicating. Now you get home from school, turn on the computer, and instantly you have ten instant messages from your ten best friends. Is there anything that would make you feel disrespected? Is there anything inconsiderate about how instant messaging works? There is. Manners are just evolving to help us use this new technology in a considerate and respectful way.

⦿ Do you feel someone is being disrespectful if she doesn't answer "instantly"?

⦿ Is it inconsiderate to get on someone else's computer and IM your best friend when you are visiting?

⦿ Does an instant message interrupt your face-to-face conversation with a friend?

⦿ Is forwarding a private message you've received the same as spreading gossip?

Apply the fundamental principles of respect, consideration, and honesty as you answer these questions, and you will know what the evolving manners should be. The standards will develop as people using instant messaging see how it affects the relationships they have with the people involved.

Text Messaging and BlackBerrys

Picture this: You are at a lecture at school and your cell phone vibrates. You flip it open and see that the call is from the friend you are meeting later. She wants to know how to get to the meeting place. You would . . .

1. Key in the directions right then.

2. Key in "text u l8r."

The respectful thing to do would be 2. It is respectful to the person giving the lecture, the others in the lecture hall with you, yourself, and your friend. The lecturer might notice you fussing with your cell phone or BlackBerry and confiscate it. The other people attending might be distracted by your activity and miss an important point, you are definitely likely to miss something important, and your friend knows you're not ignoring her and will be getting back to her in a bit.

The standards are just evolving. If they develop on the basis of our fundamental principles, they will serve to improve our communications with one another. In the long run effective guidelines for their use will increase the value these new technologies will have for all of us. They will serve to help us build and strengthen relationships.

Text Messaging: A Guide 4 U

Using your cell phone to send and receive text messages can be a great way to communicate. Just remember a few do's and don'ts and you'll be all set.

⊚ Make sure your text message ring tone is off or on silent alert if you're somewhere quiet.

⊚ Remember, your text message can always be forwarded on to other people, so be careful what you put out there.

⊚ Abbreviations: Think about your audience! Your friends all know what BTW means, but will your mom get it? LOL!

⊚ Respect your teachers and colleagues: treat texting the way you would a cell phone call, and save it until a break in class or at work.

⊚ Never try to text while you're driving. (That includes at stop lights.)

⊚ If you don't pay your own cell phone bill, check with your parents to be sure it's okay for you to send text messages, since it can cost extra—sometimes a lot extra!

⊚ Always be safe: Don't send text messages to, or receive them from, someone you don't know.

PEN AND PAPER

Are They Obsolete?

Picture this: You get home from school. Your mom yells from the kitchen, "You've got mail. It's on the table." Mail? I've got mail? The handwritten return address brings it all back. Jaimie O'Rourke. You met her at music camp last summer. She was the really cute girl who played the drums.

EIGHT TIPS FOR FOOLPROOF LETTER WRITING

1. Start with the date.

2. Follow the date by a greeting. The most common is "Dear__"

3. Spell the name of the person correctly!

4. Make sure you have the correct address.

5. Write neatly; use good grammar; check your spelling.

6. Think about what you have to say. Once it is mailed, you can't get your letter back to change it. If it's emotional, let it sit a while, and reread the letter before you send it.

7. Sign it.

8. Mail it. Keep a few stamps handy, so when you do write a letter with pen and paper, you have what you need available, and all you have to do is drop it in a mailbox.

When you all said good-bye, she said she'd write. You've been watching your e-mails and wondering, *Why nothing?* Now this . . . a letter. How cool is that?

Pen-and-paper mail carries a slightly different weight from e-mail or other electronic communications. It takes more effort. In many ways it is more substantive. The sender has taken the time to write it, address it, stamp it, and get it to the mailbox. The recipient has an active part in the communication too. He must open it, unfold it, and read it. It doesn't just appear in front of him. The physical act of sending and receiving it makes a stronger connection. Think about receiving each of the following. Which ones would mean more if they were pen and paper?

    Personal letter
    Thank-you note
    Invitation
    Business letter
    Job application letter

If you routinely communicate by e-mail, it's fine to use that as your form of communication for routine matters. But if you want to make a special impression, consider pen and paper.

Choose stationery that fits the type of letter you are writing. Personal letters can be on fun, colorful stationery. Use any color ink, and decorate the paper to fit your own style. Long letters go on letter-size stationery, and shorter correspondence can go on a card or fold-over note. However, letters written, for instance, to inquire about a job or to invite someone to be a speaker at a class event should be handwritten in black ink or printed out on white, cream, or light gray standard-size paper with minimal decoration.

Personal letters should be neatly handwritten unless your handwriting is illegible. Business letters should be typewritten. All letters should be signed by hand. And on business letters use your full name and type your name under your signature.

Respecting privacy

Whether electronic or paper, letters are private! A sealed letter is confidential and should be read only by the person it is addressed to. In days of old, people sealed their letters with personal marks set in colored wax to ensure that the letters hadn't been opened while they were en route. Some people still seal letters in wax to mark them as extra-special.

Three Key "Nevers"

⊚ Never open mail addressed to someone else— either in an envelope or on a computer.

⊚ Never read someone else's mail without permission.

⊚ Never share a letter with others that was written to you in confidence.

The Thank-You Note

When someone has given you a gift or done something special to make your life a little easier, the thank-you note is an easy way to acknowledge the time and effort he has expended on your behalf.

Remember to . . .

⊚ Write a thank-you note when you get a present and the giver is not there to receive your thanks in person (someone sends you a gift in the mail or asks someone else to bring it to you). Your thank-you note tells the person the gift arrived and how much you appreciate it.

🌀 Write a thank-you note when you have been a houseguest at someone's home. Exception: Sometimes you just go for an overnight to your best friend's house. You don't need to write a thank-you for that, but if you stay more than one night or travel to a friend's house out of town for a special event, you should write a thank-you note to your hosts.

🌀 Send a thank-you as quickly as possible, within a day or two of receiving the gift or returning home from the visit. If that's impossible, write it as soon as you can.

WHY HANDWRITE WHEN I CAN E-MAIL?

Question: My aunt sent me a great shirt for my birthday. Can I e-mail her a thank-you note?

Answer: Even though e-mail is easier, the nicest way to thank your aunt is with an old-fashioned handwritten thank-you note. If you know that your aunt checks her e-mail regularly, send her a quick e-mail to let her know that the gift arrived and you're enjoying it. Then take the time to write her a thank-you note with pen and paper. After all, she took the time to pick out the shirt, wrap it, and mail it. The e-mail note will let her know her present arrived; the thank-you note will show your appreciation and respect.

Not Required but Nice

◉ Write a thank-you note even if you've thanked the giver in person—especially if it was given at a big party and your personal thanks might have been lost in the excitement.

◉ Write a thank-you note when someone has done something special for you, say, when your uncle spent the afternoon explaining the advanced math you've been having so much trouble with.

Don't Even Think about . . .

◉ *Not* writing a thank-you note because it's late. So what if it's been two weeks? It will still show your appreciation.

◉ Using preprinted thank-you notes where you just have to fill in the blanks. The impersonal look of those cards takes away from the thought you might have put into the thank-you.

CHAPTER FOUR

The Manners and Art of Mealtime

In this chapter we'll cover:

1. The mechanics of table manners
Which fork is yours
All you need to know about your place setting
How to eat politely
2. The art of table manners
Table conversation
Traditions of mealtime

Your girlfriend's parents have invited you out to dinner. You have many questions that are making you nervous about the entire evening. What should you wear? How do you know which bread plate is yours? What if you spill your drink? You know you love spaghetti, but can you eat it without making a mess? What do you talk about since you barely know her parents? The list goes on.

TABLE MANNERS CAN MAKE A DIFFERENCE

Eating is basically a gross activity. Going out to dinner involves a variety of skills that are designed to help us enjoy the meal so we don't offend other people. Some of the skills are mechanical: holding a fork and knife correctly, drinking from your own beverage glass, spitting out the olive pit without grossing everyone out, eating spaghetti so it doesn't wind up all over your shirt. Some of the skills are social: who sits where, how you talk and eat at the same time, how you deal with a fly in your soup. There are many books written on the subject, but there is no need to memorize a bunch of rules. If you make a habit out of some basic manners, once you've learned them, you can navigate even the most formal, complicated dinner imaginable.

You celebrate many

WHY TABLE MANNERS MATTER

◆ Eating is inherently a gross activity. Table manners help keep us from disgusting the people we are with.

◆ Mechanical table manners allow us to eat any food in public with confidence.

◆ All table manners allow us to enjoy the company of others while eating.

occasions by sharing a meal: a holiday dinner with relatives, a birthday party, a date with someone special, going to a friend's dinner party, a tailgate party, your cousin's wedding banquet. The mechanics of table manners help us feel more comfortable eating with other people. The art of table manners goes to a higher level; it encompasses the social aspects of dining.

Both the mechanics and the art are integral to every shared meal regardless of formality. As with anything else, practice will help you feel more at ease in situations that really matter. You might ask, What situations really matter? You'll know when you're in one, whether it's dining out at a fancy restaurant on prom night or dinner at your new boyfriend's house. Practice at home when you're having dinner with the family, practice with your best friend at her house, and practice even when you're eating pizza with your siblings. Eventually your table manners will become second nature to you and allow you to enjoy special occasions more than ever.

AT THE TABLE

The Mechanics

Picture this: You have just won an essay contest. The local Friends of the Library club has invited you to the awards banquet to be held at a fancy hotel. You get to your seat, put your napkin in your lap, and are faced with all these questions: Which is your roll? Which glass of water should you drink from? Why do you have two forks?

At a crowded table it is hard to distinguish one setting from another. Rather than let the setting baffle you and create anxiety, look at it as a blueprint of what your meal will be. Your setting tells you at the outset whether you are having soup; whether the salad will be served before, with, or after the main course; whether hot tea or coffee will be offered; and whether the adults will be having wine. How the table is set, from an informal family meal to a formal banquet at an awards ceremony, lets everyone know what to expect.

The Family Meal

The standard place setting is typically used for one-course meals. A fork, knife, spoon, napkin, plate, and glass are all you need.

The Formal Dinner

Table settings get more complicated as the dinners get more formal. That's because there are more courses, and for each course there are different utensils and plates. At a very formal dinner you may have as many as three (sometimes even four) forks, two spoons, three knives, and four glasses. Which do you use first? There is a simple rule to follow: Just start from the outside, and work your way in with each course. If you make a mistake, don't sweat it; just apologize for taking someone's bread plate, and switch it with an unused one at the table.

The Informal Dinner: More than One Course

The informal dinner with more than one course is set for all the courses served during dinner, so there will be more utensils than at the simple family meal. You are more likely to see this setting at fine restaurants and parties or receptions where sit-down meals are served.

Let's Eat!

Bread or rolls

Either the rolls for everyone will be in a basket on the table, or one roll will be on each bread plate. If a bread basket is passed, place one roll on your bread plate along with a pat of butter. If there is no bread plate, simply put the roll and butter on the side of your dinner plate. Break off a small piece of the roll, butter it, and eat it rather than butter the whole roll at once. It can be messy to pick up the roll if it's all covered in butter!

Soup and appetizers

These will be served first. The soup spoon either is at the far right of the place setting or is brought out with the soup. Tip and move the spoon away from you as you scoop up a spoonful of soup. That way, if you spill, you won't wind up with soup in your lap. (If you tip the bowl to get that last drop, tip it away from you for the same reason.) Then sip the soup from the side of your spoon. Don't put the whole spoon in your mouth. It looks a little strange, and you are likely to dribble out of the sides of your mouth around the spoon. Try not to slurp. When you are done, leave the spoon on the plate under the soup cup or bowl. If there is no plate, leave it in the cup or bowl, but make sure the spoon is positioned so it doesn't fall out when the waiter picks it up.

Salad

Your clue to when salad will be served is the position of the salad fork, which is smaller than the dinner fork. If it is to the left of the dinner fork, your salad will be served before the main course. If it is to the right of the dinner fork, your salad will be served after the main course. If the salad is served with your main course, you won't have a salad fork. Just use the dinner fork.

The Main Course

You may know how to eat whatever is set before you; you may not. The trick here is simple: Don't go first! Watch the others at the table. You can get your clues from them about how to eat even the most difficult foods or which fork to use when. It's also good to try to match your eating speed to that of others at the table. That way you'll all finish at about the same time. Most of all, ENJOY!

TWO QUICK AND EASY TIPS FOR CUTTING

1. Whether it's a broccoli spear or piece of beef, cut a bite-size piece off your portion of food, and then eat it. Don't shove a whole huge piece into your mouth.

2. Don't cut the piece of meat into ten little pieces, and then eat them. The norm is to cut one bite at a time.

Dessert

Spoons and forks for dessert either are placed horizontally in the center above the plate or are brought to the table with the dessert. Coffee or tea is often served with dessert. If you don't care for any, just say, "No, thank you."

Q & A

Question: The dessert tonight is pie à la mode. Do I eat it with my dessert fork or spoon?

Answer: It's your choice. Some people prefer to eat ice cream with a spoon, so they eat their pie with a spoon also. Some go for the fork.

Uh-oh, What Do I Do Now?

The following are tips for handling some tricky foods:

◉ To get that last bite, use a small piece of bread or the tip of your knife blade to push the food onto your fork.

STICKY SITUATIONS: WHAT DO YOU DO WHEN . . .

◆ **You bite on something that you know is not food?** You discreetly remove it from your mouth onto your fork and then put it on the edge of your plate. If before you eat your food you see something that doesn't belong in it, remove it without comment, and place it on the edge of your plate. In a restaurant quietly tell your server about the problem, and ask for a new portion.

◆ **You have food stuck on your teeth or braces?** If you can't get it off with your tongue, excuse yourself and go to the restroom, where you can remove the food. Do not use toothpicks, floss, or your fingers to remove food from your teeth at the table.

◆ **You notice that your friend's mother has spinach stuck on her tooth?** If you know her pretty well, you can quietly tell her she has something stuck on her tooth. If you don't know her that well and would be embarrassed to say something, tell your friend, and she can quietly mention it to her mother. The point is (1) wouldn't you want someone to tell you? and (2) avoid making a big fuss about it.

◉ When cheeses are served as part of the meal, they should be cut with a knife and eaten with a fork—not with your fingers.

◉ If you have a lemon wedge for flavoring tea or

◆ **You need to sneeze, cough, or blow your nose?** Cover your mouth with a handkerchief, your napkin, or your hand. If the sneezing or coughing continues, excuse yourself, assuring the others that you are okay. You should leave the table to blow your nose. Find a bathroom, blow your nose, and wash your hands before returning to the table.

◆ **Your food is burning your mouth?** When you eat something that is too hot or too spicy, take a drink of cool water to stop the burning. If necessary, quietly spit the item back onto your fork and place it on the side of your plate without remark.

◆ **You bite into something you don't like?** If you can, it is always better to swallow what's in your mouth. Sometimes washing it down with a little water helps. If it is so bad that it is making you gag, quietly spit the item back on your fork, and place it on the side of your plate.

◆ **You spill something on the table or floor?** If you spill something, try to clean it up as completely as possible. Retrieve solid items with a spoon or knife blade, and put them on the edge of your plate. Do your best to clean up liquids with your napkin. If you are in a restaurant, ask the waiter for assistance. If you are dining at someone's home, you may help your host by getting a sponge or cloth to wipe up the spill. (If something—especially something hot—has spilled on another diner, attend to the person first and worry about the mess later.)

other beverages, either drop the wedge into the drink and press it with a spoon to get the juice out, or squeeze it directly over the drink and then drop the wedge into your drink, or put it on the side of your plate. If you squeeze the wedge, shield it with your other hand to keep from squirting others at the table.

◉ Spoon or pour ketchup for French fries onto your plate, and then dip the fries individually. French fries are considered a finger food, and you may use either your fingers or your fork to eat them. However, if they are drenched in vinegar, gravy, or ketchup, use your fork.

◉ Tacos are considered finger food and can be eaten with your fingers. However, any foodstuff that falls out of the taco as you are eating it should be eaten with a fork—not with your fingers.

◉ Pizza may be cut with a knife and eaten with a fork, but many people prefer to eat it with their fingers. You can fold the slice down the center to prevent sauce and cheese from dripping over the edges onto your hands. Stringy, melted cheese like mozzarella should be cut carefully before being lifted to your mouth, or you'll wind up with it all over your chin.

◉ When eating Asian foods, you can use either a fork or chopsticks. If there is a dipping sauce, each bite is dipped into the sauce. Do not pour the sauce over your food.

◉ Taste foods before adding seasonings; otherwise you could ruin a delicious dish that someone took great care to season just right.

◉ Remember, no double dipping in community

salsa or dips.

❾ Twirl spaghetti onto your fork using either a spoon or the side of your plate to help catch the first couple of strands for the twirl. You may also cut your spaghetti into bite-size lengths and eat it that way. The important thing is not to slurp long, dangling ends into your mouth, spraying sauce all over yourself.

THE LAST ACT

When you are finished eating . . .

◆ Leave your soup spoon on the plate or in the bowl.

◆ Leave your fork and knife on the plate in the same position a clock's hands are in at four twenty.

◆ Leave your napkin on the table (fold in any yucky stains so they don't show).

◆ Push your chair in under the table so it is out of the way.

◆ Thank the cook, the waiter, or your host.

THE ART

Meals are more than just refueling. If all you wanted was a refueling stop, you'd just grab your food from the refrigerator, heat it up (or not), fill your stomach, and be done with it. However, that's not really much fun, is it? We share meals as a way to get to know other people. Even if it's just your family, it is the time we can find out what everyone's been up to. Meals are part of many celebrations as well. The mechanics help you keep from grossing out others. The art helps you turn eating into entertaining. Some of the art is in the food itself: How does it look on the plate? Is it delicious? Some of the art is in the setting: using those blue plates that look good enough to eat. Some of the art is in the tradition: Does the menu include foods with special meaning for the diners?

Is your birthday celebrated with your favorite food? Is Thanksgiving the one time a year you use those special plates inherited from your great-grandmother? But it's even more basic than that. Whatever the occasion, whatever the celebration, whatever the menu, whatever the dinnerware, the really important thing is what happens among the people eating together. The social aspect of the meal is the most important thing.

TABLE MANNERS

The Art of Conversation

The basic ingredient for the social part of a meal is talking and listening. Good manners include the art of good conversation. Some of these basic guidelines are specific to table conversation; some of them relate to conversing anywhere. Either way, they will provide you with a blueprint for a lifetime of successful face-to-face interaction.

 ◉ Look directly at the person you are talking to.
 ◉ Listen to what is being said to you and respond appropriately.

◉ Don't interrupt.

◉ Speak clearly and slowly when it is your turn.

◉ Swallow your food before speaking. Do not talk with your mouth full.

◉ Welcome others around the table into your conversation.

◉ Avoid unpleasant topics and gross language.

◉ Keep your voice down.

◉ Remember to talk to people on each side of you.

Controversial Topics

Picture this: You are at dinner at your friend's house and her brother brings up the topic of gun control. His point of view is completely different from yours. You don't want to get into an argument with him at the dinner table. What should you do?

You can just be honest about it: *"Jim, you and I really don't agree on this issue. I'd rather not get into it here at the dinner table. Let's talk about it some other time."*

When you do find yourself in a conversation about a controversial topic, there are some things you can do to keep it civil:

- Stick to issues and facts. Take care not to offer exaggerations or facts you're not sure of. Don't say, for example, *"Thousands of murders are committed with automatic weapons,"* unless you know that to be true.

- Be diplomatic. The topic may be offensive, but it won't help you make your point any if you become offensive: *"People who think that are just so selfish. They don't care about the problem."*

- Don't be insulting. Slinging insults will only raise the emotional bar and change a conversation into an argument. *"You are so stupid. You just don't get it."*

- Don't argue. If the other person becomes offensive, let his comments pass. It's tough to argue unless both people buy into it.

- Change the subject. Probably you're not going to convince Jim to change his point of view, so you're better off talking about last night's basketball game: *"You know, Jim, I don't know if you and I will ever agree about gun control. Let's talk about something else. Did you watch that playoff game last night? It was unbelievable!"*

Dinner conversation can be a wonderful opportunity to learn about different points of view when people present their ideas in a thoughtful, nonconfrontational manner.

Small Talk

Whether you're at dinner with your family, a get-together with your friends, or a social event at school, it's easier to keep a good conversation going if you have some things to talk  about that are of general interest to all involved. Just because it's called small talk doesn't mean it's not a big deal. In the long run it's what can make you an interesting person to be with. As you get to know people better, your

---

FIVE TIPS TOWARD SUCCESS AT SMALL TALK

1. Become familiar with various topics—sports, entertainment, current events, seasonal activities—that may be of special interest to your host.

2. Ask people for their opinions.

3. Ask questions that require more than a yes or a no.

4. Listen. Listen. Listen.

5. Practice. Practice. Practice.

conversations will get deeper and will follow the paths of your common interests. But the ability to talk about general subjects helps get conversations started and will serve you well in all social encounters.

CHAPTER FIVE

School Daze

In this chapter we'll cover:

1. Basic manners for the classroom setting
2. Table manners in a unique setting, the school cafeteria
3. Beyond the classroom: friends, activities, and sportsmanship

You and a thousand other students, teachers, and staff are crammed into an eighty-year-old building, trying to fit eight hours' worth of schooling into a six-hour day. Everyone has different goals and deadlines and not enough time. Every fifty minutes a buzzer sounds, and you all have to move from one classroom into another in four minutes. Some people have their twenty-minute lunch at 10:00 A.M. and some at 2:00 P.M. because there isn't room in the cafeteria otherwise. The trick is how to make it work for everybody.

A CLASSROOM THAT WORKS

You may only have fifty minutes per class, but you all are there for the same thing. The only one with a different task, of course, is the teacher. You have a choice. You can do your part to make school pleasant for you and everyone else or not. But the mannerly thing to do would be to make it a better day for all involved.

Before Class Begins

- When you arrive in the room, greet everyone with a smile. You don't have to engage in a long dialogue. A simple hi or good morning will do.
- If there's time to talk with your friends before class, do it quietly so you don't distract others who might have last-minute studying.
- If you have last-minute studying and your friends want to talk, let them know you have something to finish and will catch up later.
- If you need to talk with the teacher about something, ask him if he has a minute before class starts. If he doesn't, schedule a time to talk later in the day.
- If someone else is talking to the teacher and

you have to wait your turn, respect her privacy by standing back a bit.

❂ Be mindful of your things. Your bags can be on the floor next to you. Leave chairs and work areas clear for people to use. Keep your book bag where no one can trip over it. Whether you are seated at a desk or table or in an auditorium, try to restrict yourself and your things to the space provided for one person.

During Class

❂ You get out of class what you put into it. Even if you're not interested in the subject at hand in general, try to find a particular aspect that you find interesting.

❂ When you have something to say, do it in the style of the class. If it's a lecture class, raise your hand when you have a question. If it's a discussion class, wait until the person speaking has finished.

❂ Follow classroom guidelines for getting up, walking around, and leaving to go to the restroom. Each teacher may have different standards.

❂ Take part in class discussions. Even if you are not talkative, you can be an active listener and show interest in what the others are saying.

❂ Sit up at your desk or table. Lying all over your desk is disrespectful to your teacher and fellow students alike. You may be tired, you may be bored, but that's no excuse for making everyone around you suffer too.

◉ Avoid passing notes or texting in class. This is just as rude as interrupting one person to start up a conversation with someone else.

PUT THE TEAM IN TEAMWORK

Question: My teacher has put me on a team with three people I don't know very well. At the end of the project we all will receive the same grade. One of the students and I seem to be doing all the work. It makes me pretty angry that the other two are just riding on our coattails. What can I do?

Answer: It's time to call a team meeting. Why not try delegating? Outline the work to be done, and assign specific tasks to each person on the team so it is clear who is doing what and by when. If that takes care of things, great. If this doesn't work, approach the teacher confidentially and ask her advice on how to handle the "slacking" students.

When Class Is Over

◉ Pick up after yourself.

◉ Move promptly out of the classroom to make room for those coming in.

◉ If you need to talk to the teacher, ask if it's a good time. Even if she's not talking to another student, she may need time to prepare for her next class. If she does, set a time to talk later.

These suggestions are about respect and consideration.

The only way the crowded, hurried atmosphere of high school is really going to work is if students and staff alike act with respect and consideration toward one another.

It's easy to act respectfully to the people you like. It's much harder to act respectfully to the ones you don't like—especially if they are not always respectful to you. Nobody likes being polite to people who don't respond in kind. It can be a real challenge, a test of your self-control and maturity.

It's particularly hard dealing with people in authority you don't like or respect. Using good manners is something that you can always be proud of in any situation. It takes confidence and self-respect to act the way you know is right despite how others may act around you.

BEYOND THE CLASSROOM

A lot goes on in the halls or locker areas and (in some schools) the student lounges and outdoor campus. Between classes, hallways can be pretty crowded, and it's hard to do anything but move with the flow. However, before school starts, perhaps during lunch periods, and after school these are the places you touch base with your friends.

One of the hardest things to remember about these shared spaces is that they are public property. They are not maintained just for you and your friends. Everyone has a right to be there. These few tips can help create an atmosphere in which everyone feels comfortable:

1. A large group walking or standing together can block the way for those who may need to get somewhere in a hurry. Make sure others can get by you comfortably.

2. Stay to the right walking down hallways, sidewalks, and stairs.

3. Slow down turning corners, and check for people coming the other way.

4. Avoid whispering and laughing in a way that makes people feel excluded or uncomfortable. Have your private conversations in private places.

5. Hold doors for others. If two or three of you get to a door at the same time, offer to let the others go first.

6. Lockers can be narrow. Take care not to block others from theirs.

7. If you're in an area where you can have snacks, pick up after yourself.

IN A CLINCH

Picture this: You go to your locker each morning to put away some of your things. The trouble is, the guy who has the locker next to yours is always in a pretty significant clinch with his girlfriend, and they block your access to your locker. You need to get into your locker, but it's embarrassing to break them up. You can . . .

> ❾ Tap one of them on the shoulder, say, *"Excuse me,"* and ask them to move. After a few days, they should get the hint.

◉ Wait until they break their clinch, and then move in quickly to your locker.

◉ If you are close friends with one of them, try talking to him when you are alone and ask him to save the clinch for somewhere else.

◉ Ask a teacher to intervene.

None of these is exactly the right thing to do. Which one you do is truly more about who you are. The couple is really putting you on the spot. Some schools have rules about public displays of affection, but both students and staff are often reluctant to do anything about it. Passionate kissing is a very private and exclusionary act. That's why it makes everyone else uncomfortable when it's done in a very public place. The important thing is for you to do what feels the most comfortable for you.

GETTING ON WITH OTHERS

Picture this: Your best friend, Marie, just told you that Amy was seen going to the movies with Sarah's boyfriend last night. Now you are at your locker and talking to Lucy. You are dying to pass on this juicy info, but you're worried that Marie could be mistaken. What should you do?

Mistaken or not, Marie might actually be guilty of starting

a rumor. Your choice is whether or not to participate in that oldest of evils: gossip. It gains nothing for anyone and can possibly cause hurt to others. Your best bet is to find something else to talk about. However, if you feel you must share the information, make absolutely certain it's true before passing it on.

CLIQUES

Small groups of people in intense conversation can make those around them feel uncomfortable. If your manner when you are with a group of friends says, "Don't approach," you might be missing something important and never know it. Cliques are exclusionary by definition. As a result, people on both sides lose. Think about how you feel when

you're excluded from an "inside" joke or people start whispering in front of you.

You don't need to be good friends with everyone—that would be impossible—but it is important to be respectful and considerate of those around you even if they're not your good friends. Gossiping and cliquishness are disrespectful and inconsiderate and prevent the development of a healthy climate.

PRIVACY

Some Things Are Nobody Else's Business

Schools, whether funded privately or by taxpayers, are by their very nature public places. That does not mean, however, that the common courtesy of respecting privacy is tossed out. It is actually even more important. People's grades, schoolwork, lockers, personal notes, and bags are not for public view. If your friend is reluctant to talk about how she did on that last exam, don't press it. Even if you are comfortable sharing your grades, she may not be, and that is her right.

While you have that same right to privacy, it is a good idea to take care with your own personal things. If you don't want someone reading your journal, keep it in your bag. Others should not read it even if they find it lying around, but curiosity has led more than one friend to read another's journal without permission. If you've lost your journal, your hope would be that someone would return it to you without reading it. Keeping the golden rule in mind, if you find a lost journal, act the way you would want that person to if the tables were turned.

Teachers Need Privacy Too

You're scheduled for a meeting with your teacher in her office. She's not there, and you have sat down to wait when you notice that her computer is on. You look at the screen and see that it is her résumé and a cover letter addressed to someone at another school. You should:

1. Avert your gaze, and keep your observations to yourself.

2. Minimize that screen. When she comes in, tell her you did that.

3. Minimize that screen. Don't tell her and figure that she'll never realize she left the screen up.

4. Read the whole thing, and let the world know she's looking for a new job.

The obvious "don't do it" answer would be 4. The trouble is that we sometimes get lured into doing something we shouldn't. That doesn't make it right. While 3 might be the most comfortable, it involves making changes on someone else's computer and it's dishonest not to tell her what you did. The honesty issue is covered by 2, but she still might be angry that you messed with her stuff. The response that is the least intrusive to your teacher and also respects her right to privacy is 1. If someone mistakenly saw something private of yours, how would you want her to act?

CAFETERIA LUNCHES

The fundamentals of table manners hold true for every meal in every setting. However, in the school setting there are other things to consider. Staff and students often need to eat in a relatively short time under very crowded conditions, so some of the fundamentals change with those circumstances. Here are the special considerations for cafeteria dining:

⦿ Help keep the line moving by picking up your food quickly and saving talk for the table.

⦿ Sit down and eat as quickly as possible. You don't need to wait for everyone to be seated before you start.

⦿ If all the tables are full, leave as soon as you are finished to make room for the next students.

⦿ Avoid asking to share food, and don't offer your food to others at the table.

⦿ Don't comment on other people's meals or eating styles. It is rude to tease a classmate who follows a special diet or brings lunch from home while others buy theirs.

⦿ Leave the table as clean as possible; dispose of trays, plates, utensils, and trash in the designated area when you leave.

⦿ Report any spills or messes to a teacher or cafeteria worker.

GETTING THERE AND BACK

It's the very start of your school day. Some students walk to school, some ride school buses, some use public transportation, some are driven in carpools by adults, some drive with their friends, and some drive themselves. Whatever your mode of travel, there are definite guidelines to follow.

Walking

⊚ Follow basic pedestrian rules: Stay on the sidewalk; cross at the lights or intersections; if there is no sidewalk, walk against the oncoming traffic.

⊚ Walk one or two abreast (unless you are on a rural road with only an occasional car).

⊚ Don't accept rides from strangers.

School Bus

⊚ Get on and off the bus quickly; cars may be tempted to pass the bus if it is stopped for a long time.

⊚ Say hello and thanks to the driver.

⊚ Don't put your things on the seat next to you.

⊚ If you have friends coming over after school, make sure that there is room on the bus you use and that they have the correct notes or permission slips to ride with you.

Public Transportation

⊚ Follow all posted rules of conduct.

⊚ Don't block doors. Get on and off quickly. It's

considerate of others who are on their way to work or school.

🌀 Be considerate of the elderly, people with disabilities, pregnant women, and moms with small children. Offer your seat to them.

🌀 Avoid taking up more than one seat.

🌀 Don't put your feet up on an empty seat or sit so that the bottoms of your shoes might touch other people.

Carpools

🌀 Be on time.

🌀 Don't eat in the car.

🌀 Leave the management of the radio dials to the person sitting in the front passenger seat.

🌀 Keep conversation reasonably quiet.

Driving

🌀 Follow all the rules of the road.

🌀 Display required permits as instructed.

🌀 Park only in places designated for students.

🌀 During the school day, follow all school driving regulations, such as how many other students may ride in your car.

Getting to and from school both starts and ends your day. It can set the mood for all that follows. A little consideration for those around you will make it easier for everybody. You have the power to decide what kind of day it's going to be or has been. Use that power to your best advantage.

CHAPTER SIX

Getting a Job or Getting into College

In this chapter we'll cover:

    1. Manners that are important in getting, doing, and keeping a job

    2. Manners that are important in applying to colleges

It's time to leave for the interview. You spent hours figuring out the best outfit, you've showered and dressed, you're well rehearsed, and you know you can nail this one. As you pass through the kitchen, you decide to have that last swallow of coffee, and you manage to spill it all over yourself. You can change and be late in an outfit that wasn't your first choice, you can go to the meeting and hope the interviewer doesn't notice, or you can grab a sweater and be on time with the layered look. What would you do?

BEFORE THE INTERVIEW

You'd like some extra pocket money, and you've decided you need a job. Before you do anything, you need to make some decisions. Ask yourself the following questions:

How much time do you have? (During the school year you need to be sure that you will be able to honor whatever commitment you make to the job while honoring your commitment to school. For a summer job, time may still be an issue.) Are you going on a summer trip with your family? Do you participate in summer theater, or are you in a summer sports league? Are you willing to commit to getting up at 7:00 every morning during your vacation in order to get to an 8:00 A.M. job?

How far away is the job? Do you have transportation to get there?

What are your skills? Do you live at the mall? Can you type? Do you have the knack for food service or preparation? Do you have special training to be a lifeguard or camp counselor? Can you drive a tractor and bale hay? Are you looking for an internship in a profession that interests you?

What are your personal likes and dislikes? Before you apply for a job at a child care center, consider how it might be to spend all day with a group of two- and three-year-olds. If you love being outdoors, you might want to look for jobs that won't bind you to an office. Remember that you'll be working for several hours at a time, and it will be so much  easier if you actually like your job and what you're doing.

After you've decided on the kinds of jobs you want to go for, you can begin the process of applying. The first step may be a phone call, in which case you want to think about some basic phone manners that will help you make a good first impression.

1. Identify yourself: *"Hello, my name is Mary Hama and—"*

2. State your reason for calling: *"I am interested in the job for a lifeguard that you advertised in the local paper."*

3. Speak clearly.

4. Be prepared to follow through promptly with whatever instructions you get on the phone.

5. Keep a smile on your face. Even if the person answering can't see the smile, he will "hear" it.

Whether you make the first contact in person, in writing, or over the phone, you will need to fill out an application and may even need to prepare a cover letter and résumé. More often than not, it's the written documents that will create your very first impression.

⊚ If it is an application form, fill in all the spaces provided. Use black or blue ink, and print clearly and legibly.

⊚ It's good to have more than one application handy so if you make an error, you can redo it.

⊚ If you need to attach a cover letter and résumé and you have access to a computer and printer, use them.

⊚ Check spelling and grammar carefully, and ask someone to proofread your work for you.

⊚ Be sure your written work is projecting the right image. You are selling yourself here and want to get in for that all-important interview. If your application form or letter is messy or incomplete, an employer may not even bother to meet you. It's not only respectful to make the extra effort but smart!

You may need to provide names of people who will serve as references for you. Some could be people who know you personally, like teachers, coaches, a local religious leader, a drama director. Some could be work-related: prior bosses (don't forget the family down the street for whom you've baby-sat or done yard work for years). You want to choose as references people who will speak highly of you. Before putting anyone's name down, ask her if it's okay: "Hi, Mrs. Gupta. I'm applying for a job at the local gym. Can I put you down as a reference?" Let her know what it entails: "The person at the gym will call," or she may have to fill out a form you will provide. (If it is a form, provide a stamped, addressed envelope.) That's all it takes.

THE ALL-IMPORTANT INTERVIEW

You've done it! The manager at the gym has called to ask you in for an interview. This is your opportunity to let him know who you are and that you could do a great job for him. The following checklist can help you make it a successful interview:

🕘 **Be early!** You may have to wait a few minutes. Use that time to compose yourself, think about what you want to get across, and

TIMING IS EVERYTHING

You want to be early, but not too early. Fifteen minutes is just about right. More than that and the interviewer may not know what to do with you. Less than that plus missing the bus might make you late. If your appointment is at rush hour, you'll want to leave additional travel time. If you're not sure how long it takes to get there, make a practice run so you can make your timing perfect.

review any questions you want to ask. Leave yourself enough time for any unforeseen circumstances—spilling coffee all over yourself or a traffic jam, for instance.

⑨ **Be ready!** Have all pertinent information about yourself in order. Think ahead about the qualifications you have that fit well with the position. Consider how you will answer common interview questions like, Why do want this job? What have you done that has prepared you for this job? What special skills do you have?

⑨ **Be prepared!** Plan the questions you want to ask. If there is information readily available that you can get ahead of time about the job, get it. Use the valuable time of the interview for information you can't get elsewhere.

⑨ **Dress appropriately!** If you are interviewing for a job at the local clothing store, you'll choose one outfit; if the job is a pool-cleaning job, you might choose a different one. In either case, your clothes should be clean, neat, without holes, and well fitted. (See pages 26–31 for discussion about image.)

⑨ **Speak clearly!** Even if you are very shy, it is important to speak clearly and loudly enough that the interviewer doesn't have to ask you to repeat everything. Avoid mumbling. Look at the interviewer when you speak. That gives him some visual cues—your facial expression, your lips moving—that help clarify what you are saying.

⑨ **Shake hands twice!** Once when you arrive and once when you leave.

⑨ **Thank the interviewer twice!** Once verbally when you leave and once in writing.

MAKING THE DIFFERENCE

You've made the proverbial short list of final job candidates. A well-written and timely thank-you note might be just the thing to make you stand out from the other applicants. Two important tips to make the thank-you note work for you:

1. Mail it the next day so the interviewer gets it while you are fresh in her mind.

2. Keep it short. Three or four sentences are enough. This is a thank-you, not a note to make your case for yourself.

Dear Mrs. Mancia,

Thank you very much for taking the time to meet with me yesterday. It sounds like you have a great team working at The Fitness Space, and I would love to be on it. Do let me know if you need any other information from me. I'm looking forward to hearing from you.

Thank you again,

Mark McAllister

KEEPING THE JOB

You got it! All your planning and care with the application process have paid off. Getting the job was step one. Now the trick is to prove yourself and to do the job well. It is essential that you honor all your commitments either expressed or implied by your accepting the job:

- To work the number of hours assigned to you
- To arrive and leave on time
- To perform all the tasks associated with your job to the best of your ability—even the boring or unpleasant ones
- To treat coworkers and clients with respect and consideration
- To represent well the company or person that hired you

You have the opportunity not only to make some money but also to gain valuable experience that will help you get the next job you apply for. It's a classic double bind that you need experience to get a job, but you can't get that experience if no one will hire you because you don't have experience. So if you've cracked that nut and gotten that first job, make the most of it.

COLLEGE BOUND?

The checklist for a successful job interview also applies

at the college interview. The only thing that changes is content. You may

want to focus on the skills you have that will serve you well in an academic setting. Your questions should relate to the college, not the job, and have a different slant. But the steps are the same, right down to the thank-you note.

The college interview is certainly critical, but there are several other components of the college application that are significant and require equal attention from you. Most college applications require at least one essay, a cover letter, and one- or two-sentence answers to some shorter questions. It is important that all these be the best you can do in content, as well as grammatically correct, free from spelling errors, legible, and without extraneous smudges and ink marks. As with the job application, make a copy of the blank application, so if you make a mistake, you have a clean copy you can use. Some colleges offer application forms online. If you apply via the computer, print out the completed application, and proofread it carefully before you submit it.

Colleges usually ask you to send references. There is often a form to be used for the reference. When you ask a teacher or employer to provide a reference, give her the form and let her know of any deadlines you have. The college may ask that the reference be sent directly to it, in which case you should also provide the person you are asking with an addressed, stamped envelope. Teachers and guidance counselors have many requests for references, so think carefully about whom you are asking. The person should be someone who knows you well enough to write about you with conviction. Pick people who can attest positively to your character and abilities. After the application has been completed and all the materials have been sent in, it is appropriate to write short notes thanking your references for taking the time to speak on your behalf. When you hear from the college, make it a point to let the people who have written references know how you fared in the application process.

Jobs and college represent your first steps toward adult independence. For both, you are putting yourself out there and saying, "This is who I am. Choose me for your organization." So take your time with your applications and interviews. Make your best effort so that you will be judged on who you are. And when you are entrusted with a job or college acceptance, keep in mind that you are the one in control of how well you ultimately do. These are your own opportunities to make it or not, and they will be the building blocks for your ultimate success when you are out there truly on your own.

CHAPTER SEVEN

Social Savvy

In this chapter we'll cover:

1. Being a host; being a guest

2. The etiquette of proms and other parties

3. When dating is not outdated

The big event is fast approaching. So many questions. Do you go with a group, or do you work on getting a date? What will you wear? How will you get there? If the party is at your house, whom do you invite?

YOU'RE THE HOST

Come On Over to My House

There are so many occasions to have people over. It can be one or two friends just hanging out; it can be a party with twenty friends; it can be a group of eight meeting to go to the prom together; it can be a sweet sixteen or *quinceañera* party. Whatever the event, there are some things you can do that will make it a good time for everyone there.

When the 'Rents Are MIA

You want to have some friends over. But your parents are going away the weekend you've chosen.

1. You get the word out that they're away and it's an open house at 222 Twentieth Street.

2. You plan to hold the party somewhere else.

3. You plan to have the party when your parents can be around.

4. You see if you can get your uncle Bob to be around and have the party with your parents' knowledge.

5. You ask them. Remind them they know they can trust you, and have the party with their permission.

The only really wrong choice would be 1. All the others reflect a sense of respect, consideration, and honesty. Those are the core principles that should drive any choice. If you want your parents to treat you with respect, consideration, and honesty, you need to return the favor. It might not always let you do things exactly as you'd like, but it will strengthen your relationship with your parents and your friends.

DECIDING WHOM TO INVITE

Deciding whom to invite is the trickiest, most difficult part of planning a get-together. You don't want hurt feelings; you need to limit numbers; you have tons of friends. What to do?

◆ Think about numbers.

◆ Think about the things you'll be doing and who would most enjoy them.

◆ Think about people who will get along.

◆ Think about adjusting the size of the party so you don't have to cut the list in an awkward place.

Plan

Impromptu can be good, but it also can leave you open to problems. A little planning can go a long way to make even the most informal gathering a success. You do have choices, and all it takes is some time and thought to pick what will work for you.

◎ How many people are you asking over?

◎ Who will they be?

◎ What activities will take place?

◎ Will you have food and drinks available?

◉ When will it start; when will it end?

◉ Is transportation an issue?

Invite

The type of invitation depends in large part on the event. Friends over after school probably just need a phone call or a personal verbal invitation at school. A group over to watch a movie might get a phone call or an e-mail invitation. A sweet sixteen party definitely warrants an official written invitation: "Please come over to my house for a Sweet Sixteen Party on

Q & A

Question: A friend of mine called me to invite me to a party at her house. But before she asked me, she asked what I was doing this weekend. I said, "Nothing much," which was true. The thing is I don't really want to go to the party, but once I said I was doing nothing, it was really hard to say no. What should I have done?

Answer: Your friend put you in a difficult position by asking what you were doing before she invited you to her party. She should have invited you first.

That being said, the only thing you could have said was, "You know, thank you so much for inviting me, but I really am committed to keeping this a nothing-much weekend. I have been so incredibly busy. I've really wanted an evening to do nothing, and this is my only chance." There is no obligation for you to say yes to an event you don't want to attend. The important thing is to be honest so you don't get caught up in a false excuse.

Saturday, May 3, from 7 to 11. RSVP 555-4567."

Send invitations to home addresses rather than deliver them at school. That way you will avoid hurting the feelings of those you haven't invited. Think how you'd feel if you saw friends handed party invitations at school and didn't get one yourself.

Prepare

If you're having friends over to study for an exam, pick up your room so everyone has a place to sit comfortably with the stuff you're studying spread around. Don't have everyone over to watch the Super Bowl if your only working TV has a nine-inch screen. If you're having a party to celebrate your best friend's birthday, be sure you have the time you need to prepare food and bake or buy that cake she wants. Talk with your mom about who's doing what, so your crisis doesn't become hers. And if your parents haven't agreed to foot the bill, make sure you can afford to pay before you party. The more preparation you do beforehand, the more time you'll actually have to spend having fun with your friends.

Keep Your Eyes Peeled

It's your job as host to see that everyone you've invited over has a good time. Greet people as they arrive. If you see someone sitting alone, make the effort to talk to him and try to start him socializing. If you see two friends getting into an argument, step in and help them change the subject. Make sure there is plenty of food and drink available for everyone. If half your guests are vegans, you'll want to serve something besides burgers. Take care not to hang with the same people and leave the others out. If people are partying too heartily, don't hesitate to ask for some help from the adults in the house. As people leave, be sure to thank each one for coming.

Afterward

If you've had a big party, maybe you can invite one or two of your closest friends to stay after and help clean up. If it's just a few of your friends over, ask them to help pick up before they leave. In any case, pick up after yourself. You cannot expect your parents, siblings, or roommates to clean up after you, which brings us to . . .

YOUR PARENTS, SIBLINGS, AND ROOMMATES

Never forget it is their house too. How will your activities affect them? Do your parents have rules about whom you can ask over and when? Does your roommate have a big exam tomorrow? Will your dad join you to watch the big game, or

are you expecting him to hand over the remote and leave?
There are no set rules except the ones that require you to be
considerate and respectful of the others you share your home
with. As you plan your event, always take them into
consideration.

YOU'RE THE GUEST

Going Over to a Friend's House

Here are some guidelines for you to follow when you're
the guest rather than the host.

> ❧ It begins with your choice about going. If you
> don't want to go, don't. You don't have to make
> up excuses. You simply say, "No thanks, but
> thanks for asking." There is no obligation to
> explain.

> ❧ Arrive and leave at the times on the invitation.
> Being late is all about choices. If you aren't sure
> about the time, check it with your host.

> ❧ What's your mood? It's entirely up to you
> whether you wear a smile or a frown. If you find
> yourself sinking into a bad mood, find things you
> can enjoy about the party. Concentrate on them.
> If you focus on the negative, it will affect not only
> your enjoyment but the enjoyment of those
> around you.

> ❧ Help out. Offer to pass around some food or
> refill cups. If you see someone sitting alone, go
> engage the person in conversation. If you know

how to fix the DVD player, step in and offer
your help. And when the party's
almost over, you can always offer to
help with the cleanup.

◉ Express appreciation. Be sure
to say thank you as you leave. For
ending an event on a high note,
nothing else can compete with a genuine
expression of appreciation. A quick e-mail
the next day to say what a nice time you had is
also a great gesture.

WHEN THINGS GET WEIRD

Picture this: You are at a party at a friend's house. One of
the other guests approaches you and says, "Hey, come on.
Jake got hold of some beer. He's outside by the garage with
Marie and Doug." You really don't want to go. You would . . .

◉ Join them anyway and just have a few sips.
After all, you don't want to seem like a nerd.

◉ Say, "No, thanks," and stay inside to continue
enjoying the party.

◉ Say, "No, thanks, I'm not really a beer drinker. You
shouldn't be either. You could get in big trouble."

◉ Say, "No, thanks," and let your friend whose
house it is know about the beer drinking going on
out by the garage.

◉ Say, "No, thanks," call your parents—"I'm not
really having a great time here. Could you come

SAYING NO IS EASY

You start with "No, thanks."

Your friend presses: "Why can't you come?"

Depending on which is true, you can say . . .

◆ "It's just not a good time for me. I have more on my plate than I can handle right now."

◆ "I'm really not into action movies" (or horror movies, or space movies, or playing ball, or dancing, or whatever it is).

◆ "I'm spending all weekend studying for the calculus exam" (or writing a paper, or reading that book for English lit).

The key is to be honest. Find the positive "I'd really like to but . . ." and give an honest negative. If you just don't like the person inviting you, skip the positive intro, and leave it at the no stage. If pressed, you can just say "no, thank you" again. If you say no several times, it's likely she'll stop asking.

get me?"—and let your friend know about the beer drinking and that you're heading home.

The right answer depends on you. You need to consider all the issues associated with the legality of what's going on and whether or not you personally want to be implicated. (If you are at a party with illegal liquor or drugs, you can still get in trouble, even if you didn't have any yourself.) And you need to be respectful and honest with your host. It's a big responsibility, and the choice can be difficult. The important thing is to act consistently with who you are and what you believe.

UP-TO-DATE DATING

Dating? Who dates anymore anyway? You may have had a boyfriend or girlfriend for years and never have gone out on a date. You've gone to each other's houses to share food, TV, music, and computers; you've gone to events at the school like proms and winter festivals; and you've gone out together with your friends. But you may not have gone out on an actual date. While it is not as common as it used to be, there are still opportunities for dates, and they can make for a special evening.

Picture this: Your cousin is a dancer with a national dance troupe. It is coming to a city near you in six weeks. He has sent you two tickets for the performance. There is a new guy in your math class at school you have become friendly with. You think it might be a great occasion to get to know him a little better.

1. You would give him a call and ask him to join you.

2. You would talk to him after math class, let him know you've been given two tickets, and ask him to join you.

3. You would ask a mutual friend to ask him for you.

4. You would offer to sell him one of the tickets and then just show up sitting next to him at the performance.

If you're really interested in an opportunity to get to know him a little better, 1 and 2 are the only choices for you. You certainly don't want to have a friend deliver a note or ask on your behalf (3). It might look as though you don't have the confidence to speak for yourself, and you might not really want the other person to know if you are turned down! Now, 4 speaks for itself. You may get to sit next to him for the performance, but you've probably done nothing to up your chances for building a relationship.

Asking Someone Out on a Date

There are some guidelines to consider once you've decided to ask someone out. Whether it's a dance, a concert, or the football game this weekend, these six tips will make the act of asking a bit easier:

1. Ask early. For a casual date to the movies, two to four days is fine. For a concert or event that requires ordering tickets in advance, ask before you buy the tickets.

2. Call or ask in person. Avoid sending a note through a friend or having someone else ask for you.

3. Use good timing. If you're calling, avoid dinnertime or phoning after 9:00 P.M. Also, avoid interrupting someone who's talking to friends to ask him out.

4. Be specific. Let the person know exactly why you're calling: "Hi, I was planning on going to the concert next Friday. Would you like to join me?" Don't start by asking, "What are you doing next Friday?"

SAYING YES OR NO

When it's yes: A "blah" acceptance might give the message that you feel "blah" about the invitation. An enthusiastic yes will give the impression that you feel good about the invitation.

When it's no: Be honest. You don't have to be specific, but you do have to be honest.

If you are asked out by someone you don't want to date, "Sorry, I already have plans for Friday" will suffice.

If it's someone you would like to go out with, you can be more specific: "I'm really sorry I can't say yes. It's my grandmother's birthday, and we've planned a special family party for her that night. I'd love to go out another time if we can work it out."

Both are honest replies; only one is specific.

5. Be ready with details. If the answer is yes, be prepared to talk about times, transportation, what to wear, and any other specifics.

6. Decide who pays. It's important to be clear about this. If you are not prepared to pay for the entire evening, say so up front: "I've got the tickets to the concert covered, but if we want to eat first, it would have to be dutch treat."

Being Exclusive

You've met that special person who also thinks you are pretty special. The next thing you know you are "going together." As with so many things, there are definite advantages and disadvantages to pairing off. Before you really get linked with that one special person, you might want to consider:

Advantages

- You don't have to worry about getting a date for the prom.
- You can feel at ease with someone.
- You really get to know that person better.
- It "proves" your feelings for the other person.
- It makes you feel attractive.
- Everybody does it.

Disadvantages

- You are out of circulation.
- It can be boring.

◎ You can get too involved.

◎ You can feel pressured to have sex.

◎ It can tie you down.

◎ It's really tough when one of you decides to break up.

◎ Everybody does it.

Breaking Up Is Really Hard to Do

Sometimes romantic feelings just fade down to a comfortable friendship. When that's the case, it's pretty easy to break up.

It's also a pretty rare occurrence. It's more likely that one person in the relationship wants to end it while the other doesn't. That can be tough. The critical thing in this situation is to be honest, do it face-to-face, be sure there's time to talk, be sure it's private, and be sensitive to the fact that it may be painful for both of you. Take care with what you say and how you say it. Most important, don't talk about it with the rest of the world. Put yourself in the other person's place. How would you want to be treated? Certainly not as the subject for gossip. It is important that you wind up the relationship with a sense of respect both for the other person and for yourself.

If someone is breaking up with you, express your emotions, but don't let them get control of you. Let him know, but take care not to say things you'll regret later, when emotions have cooled a bit. It's natural to feel sadness and anger at first. Deal with your emotions in a way that is most helpful for you. Go for a run or bike ride, buy those shoes you've wanted, have a coffee at your favorite café, or talk to your best friend about how you're feeling. An outward appearance of "It's been great, but I'm glad to be on my own again" will get you through the worst of it. Time is a great healer, and while it seems impossible at the moment, "this too shall pass." If after a while the sadness and anger don't go away, consider talking about it with an adult you trust. Who knows? She may have been there herself.

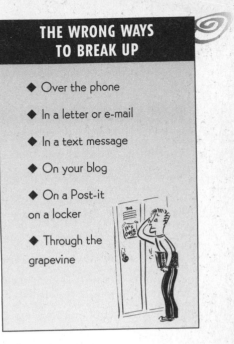

THE WRONG WAYS TO BREAK UP

◆ Over the phone

◆ In a letter or e-mail

◆ In a text message

◆ On your blog

◆ On a Post-it on a locker

◆ Through the grapevine

SEX: THE PRESSURE IS ON—OR IS IT?

Does being sexy necessarily equate with having sex? Maybe not. There does appear to be a lot of pressure—especially on girls—to look and act sexy. Skirts may be really short, or not; navels may be exposed, or not; necklines may plunge below the waist, or not; pants may be really tight, or not. Styles come and go. Some are sexy, and some are not.

Are the fashion designers selling sex or selling a product? Does sex sell? These are important questions because the answers may help shape your behavior. The important thing is that you ask yourself these questions. If sex—and this includes oral sex—is really an expression of your love for someone, truly a giving of yourself to another, then it is not something you do because . . .

- Everyone else is doing it.
- You want to prove you really are sexy.
- You want to be loved.
- You are curious about how it feels.
- You think the person you're going with will break up with you if you don't.

There are some questions you can ask yourself before making a decision to have sex:

- Is everyone else really doing it or just talking big?
- Would I be able to look this person in the eye the next morning and talk about the experience?
- If it doesn't go that well, will I feel hurt, embarrassed, angry, or used?
- If we break up afterward anyway, how will I feel about myself?
- Am I willing to buy and use condoms?
- What if this experience results in an STD (sexually transmitted disease) or a pregnancy?
- Do I really trust this person?

🌀 Do I really love this person, and does that make a difference?

🌀 Is this the only way to prove my love?

Sex is the most intimate act between two people, so you should take the time to consider all these questions and answer them coolly and honestly—not in the heat of the moment. Most important, make your own decisions. Don't let someone or something else make them for you.

THE PROM AND OTHER PARTIES

Homecoming, winter carnival, Valentine's Day, *Cinco de Mayo*, the prom, and graduation are party times that occur throughout the school year. Your school may have any or all of them. They are a great opportunity to dress up, eat, dance, and have a special evening with your friends and classmates. They are special because they may occur only once (at most three or four times) in your high school experience. All the same, you will enjoy these special times even more if you know what to expect.

🌀 **Do I need a date?** At some events you may be more comfortable with a date. If you are not planning to go with someone special, think about pairing up with a good friend. Make your plans early enough so you don't wind up dateless a week or two before the event. You may want to get a special dress or rent a tuxedo, and that is hard to do the week before a big party.

⊚ Can I go with a group? A good alternative to going with a date is to go with a group of your friends—same sex or mixed. You can enjoy all the fun of the party without some of the pressures of having a date.

⊚ Do I buy flowers for my date? Yes, in most cases. The guy should ask his date the color of her dress, so he can get flowers that match. If you get a wristlet (a corsage with elastic that can be put on her wrist) or a nosegay (a small bouquet that is carried), you can avoid having to pin the corsage to the dress. If you do get a corsage, it can be pinned at the waist, high on her shoulder, or on her evening bag. The florist can help with your selection. The girl usually gets a small boutonniere for her date. A rose or carnation looks handsome on a tuxedo.

PIN IT ON

Hold the flower in place. Insert the pin down through the fabric. Push it up through the fabric, then through the flower stem, and back down through the fabric. For a heavier corsage you may want to use two crisscrossed pins to hold the flower more securely. As with any skill, a little practice helps. Try pinning a corsage on your mom, sister, or brother before the big party so you'll seem like a pro when it comes to the big event.

⊚ How will we get there? The prom may be the one event of your high school career for which you can rent a limo. Check out the car companies, find out the prices and how many people can fit in, figure out who might want to join you, and work out the prices early in the game. If the limo idea isn't for you, decide who will drive: you, an older sibling, your parents, or a friend. Keep in mind that whoever agrees to drive is also agreeing to stay sober! If the driver does end up drinking, it is not only your choice but your obligation to find another way home.

⊚ Do we have to go out for dinner? No, although many couples do go out to restaurants before going to the prom. If you're on a budget, you might want to plan dinner at someone's house instead of going out. Or consider a less expensive restaurant. The idea is to have a good time, not to break the bank. You and your date or group of friends should do what works best for you all. If you do plan to go to a restaurant, it is a good idea to call ahead and make a reservation, so you don't wind up having to wait hours for a table and miss the dance. If you have dinner at someone's house, plan ahead who is taking care of preparation and cleaning up.

⊚ Is there always a party after the dance? Find out before the dance what the after-dance options are. Is everyone checking into a hotel? Is there a party at someone's house with parents around? Is the group going to a beach where there will be a keg? You can make your choice. If you don't want to go to the party after the dance, be sure you have arrangements for getting home. It may feel a little awkward, but if you'd rather just go home for pizza and some rehashing of the dance, that's what you should do. The best plan is the one that keeps you in control of your own decisions and shows respect for yourself and the people you are with. Use your common sense.

CHAPTER EIGHT

Out and About

In this chapter we'll cover:

1. Mall manners
2. Dinner out: fast food or sit down
3. We've got tickets!
4. Driver's ed
5. The good sport

MALL MANNERS

You and a friend are standing in a long line at the local fast-food place in the mall. Two other friends come up and ask if they can join you in the line. Your friend says, "Sure!"

YOU'RE RIGHT, IT'S NOT FAIR

Sometimes an adult may see a group of high school students and think the worst. The adult may not be reacting to you but to the teen who was rude to her a few minutes before. Not fair? You're right, it's not fair. But that's the reality. And just about the only thing you can do is to try to change that adult's image of a high school student and be the best person you can be. After her experience with you, what will she think the next time she meets a teen?

and they cut into the line with you. You notice glares from the people behind you. And you can understand why they are glaring. There isn't always an easy answer: You can say something to your friend, who doesn't think there's anything wrong with asking the others to join you, you can say something to the others, who wouldn't be thrilled about going to the end of the line, or you can smile awkwardly at the people behind you.

People can think very differently about what's okay behavior, and that can create some tense situations. Your only option is to commit yourself to acting in a way that doesn't add to someone else's tension.

Nearly everyone has experienced an afternoon at the mall, shopping, eating, playing video games, going to the movies, and just being with friends. The tricky thing is that there are crowds of other people there with the same plan: to shop, eat, or just be with friends or family. Malls are no different from other public spaces, and the manners are the same there as they are in school or anywhere else. Here's a refresher of the top five manners for sharing space:

1. Make room for other people. If you are with a group of friends, walk two or at most three across. Stay to the right, and if a walkway is narrow, step back a little to let those coming the other way go by you.

2. Use those famous "magic" words. Say excuse me, thank you, and please to your friends, other shoppers, and clerks. The "magic" is that you can make people feel good and have a better day with just one or two words.

3. Keep it down. If you notice that your group is getting loud, start talking in a quiet voice. It's amazing how people follow suit. Try it. Talk to someone in a whisper, and he is apt to whisper back.

4. Use only the tables, chairs, and space you need. Your backpack may be taking up a seat that others could use for a person at their table. Keep your things within a reasonable space near where you are sitting, so you can keep an eye on them and avoid tripping someone else.

5. Pick up after yourself. Clear your trash, put tables and chairs back where you found them, and wipe up any spills.

Just use your basic good manners. Say good morning to the clerks at the stores, open doors for others, put things back on shelves and racks as you found them, wait your turn patiently if all the clerks are busy, find an out-of-the-way corner to make your quick cell phone call, and, most important of all, try to think about others as well as yourself.

WHAT DO YOU DO?

You are in the bookstore. You have an hour to spare and are looking forward to browsing in your favorite section. But then you realize someone is following you. You test it out. Sure enough, as you move up and down the aisles, a store clerk is moving along with you. What do you do?

1. Do you say something to her? If you choose to say something, the important thing is to be neither defensive nor aggressive: "Excuse me, miss, is there a problem?"

2. Do you continue with your browsing and ignore her? It is perfectly polite to ignore the clerk in this situation.

3. Or do you leave and do your shopping at a store where you feel welcome? It's your money to spend. You decide where you want to spend it.

How do you know whether or not to call an adult by his proper title and last name or by his first name? The guideline here is simple. You address an adult by her title and last name—unless she specifically asks you to use her first name or something else. If you are introducing someone your age to an adult, use the adult's title and last name. Let the adult make the choice of whether or not to request something different: "Dad, this is my friend Samantha. Sam, this is my father." Your father may choose to say, "Hi, Sam, please call me Jack. All the kids do." Or he might simply say hello to Sam and not comment on his name, meaning that he wants Sam to call him Mr. Chen.

MR., MRS., MS., DR., OR FIRST NAMES

Question: Last week I was at the mall with my friend. We were having lunch with her father. When she introduced me, I called him Mr. Iannelli, and he asked me to call him Bill. The trouble is that my mother insists I call adults by their titles and last names. What should I have done?

Answer: You have two options. One, you could have said, "It's great to meet you, Mr. Iannelli. I hope you don't mind if I call you Mr. Iannelli. My mom is quite adamant that I call adults Mr. or Mrs." Two, you could have called him by his first name as he requested and then later talked with your mother about how you should handle that situation in the future.

Also difficult and sometimes confusing is running into your teacher in a setting outside school. What if you are at a local rock band concert and there is your teacher and her boyfriend? Do you talk to her? What if you find yourself dancing next to her? In a school setting she has some control and authority over you. In this setting she does not. However, she will take her impressions of you back to the schoolroom with her, just as you will take your impression of her along with you. With luck you both will treat each other with the consideration and respect you use in the classroom. You certainly should greet her, and any conversation should relate to the event: "Great band! I didn't know you liked this group." Stay away from topics related to your teacher/student relationship. Don't say, "I hope you liked the essay I just turned in." Two important tips that might help you deal with this potentially awkward situation:

1. While she is not grading you on your behavior, she will form an impression based on how you act. What impression would you want her to have?

2. Keep in mind that her private social life is her own and not food for gossip at school.

EATING OUT

Whether you are in a fast-food restaurant or sitting in a restaurant with menus, wait staff, and check at the end of the meal, there are manners that will help you have a successful experience. (Remember to use all the table manners noted in Chapter Four no matter where you are, except in the few instances noted below.)

Waiting

Sometimes you will wait in line (to order or to have a seat), and sometimes you will wait for your food to be served. Patience is not always easy when you're hungry, but if the kitchen is backed up, there is little the person serving you can do, and an impatient or angry comment will only make things more uncomfortable. If it seems you've been waiting unreasonably long, you may ask the server how much longer she expects it will be. If you notice long lines when you arrive, it is okay to ask how long it may take to be served, and you can opt not to eat there if the time frame doesn't work for you.

While in line or sitting at the table with a menu, take time to decide what you want to order before conversing with your friends. When the server arrives (or it's your turn), speak clearly so the server gets it the first time. If you are placing the order for several people, get it straight ahead of time so you can order without confusion. If you are in a food court and pick up your food before others do, you may begin eating when you get to the table. You don't have to wait for all your friends to return to the table with their meals.

If you are meeting people at a restaurant, you should wait until everyone has arrived to place your order (except for beverages, which you may order while waiting for the others). If your food is served first, you should wait to start until several others at the table have their meals. If the delay is long, ask the others if you may eat so your food doesn't get cold.

Tipping

In a fast-food place where you provide all your own service, there is no need to tip.

At a restaurant where a waiter is taking your order, serving your food, and clearing the table you should leave a tip of 15 to 20 percent of the total cost of the meal (pretax).

If you are at a buffet (where you select your meal from a table with many dishes on it) and the staff sets the table and clears your dirty dishes when you get up for more food, you should leave a 10 percent tip.

In restaurants where there is a sign asking you to wait to be seated, you do not need to tip the person who leads you to a table.

Wherever you are eating, you should turn off your cell phone. If you need to use it to contact someone regarding rides and meeting places or to have some other short communication, go somewhere out of the dining area so other people don't have to overhear your phone call while eating.

WE'VE GOT TICKETS!

You may be at the neighborhood movie theater or you may be at a once-in-a-lifetime concert. In either case you are looking forward to enjoying the show. You probably do not want to listen to a group of kids talking loudly about last night's party, who's going with who, or any other topic. If you are comfortable doing so, you may ask the others to be quiet. If you do it respectfully and reasonably, that may be all it takes. If they are arrogant, nasty, or paying no attention to you, you may have to ask an usher in the theater to deal with them. You should never set yourself up for a confrontation. It is the job of those who work there to take care of problem patrons. A few other things you should avoid that can be disruptive for others in a theater include:

- Letting friends join you in the ticket line in front of others who have been waiting.
- Arriving late so you have to cross over in front of others after the show has begun.
- Constantly getting up and down and walking

in front of others.

◉ Not turning off your cell phone. If you must have the phone on for some reason, it should be set to vibrate, not ring.

◉ Leaving a mess—popcorn containers, soda cups, candy wrappers—all around your seat.

◉ Standing on your seat and blocking the view of those behind you.

DRIVER'S ED

Finally! You've waited your whole life for this. You studied for the written exam; you drove with your parent in the car as long as required by state law; you took hours of driver's education; you practiced parallel parking thirty-five times until you got it right; you took your test; and now you have your driver's license.

This is a huge responsibility. There is road rage to contend with, there are negligent drivers out there, there are variable weather conditions, there are many different road conditions, and you are in control of a vehicle that can seriously injure and even kill.

One sixteen-year-old tells the story of seeing a truck bearing down on him as he was on a patch of ice and had no control. All he could think about was how he would tell his friend's parents that their son, his

RESPONSIBLE DRIVING

Focus on driving. If you are with your friends, your responsibility to drive safely is more important than paying attention to the person talking. Watch out for pedestrians, cyclists, and pets. Especially watch out for small children.

friend in the passenger seat, was dead. Fortunately the truck driver was in control and veered out of the way, and the only damage was to the car. The friend was not hurt. The sixteen-year-old had nightmares for weeks.

Some of the basic principles of etiquette can help you handle driving with the maturity it deserves:

1. Consideration for and awareness of the others on the road are key to driving safely.

2. Leave your temper at home. Using a car to express your anger can only lead to tragedy.

3. Use good manners 24/7. They are not something to be turned on and off. They are for use every day all day. That goes for in the car too.

Picture this: You are driving to an important interview for a summer job. Traffic is heavy. Someone cuts you off; you honk your horn and make a rude gesture. Two hours later, when you meet the interviewer, you realize you've seen him before, that same day on the highway. That rude gesture has come back to haunt you!

The Polite Passenger

When you are riding with others, there are several manners that will help keep everyone safer. While your mother may not hesitate to ask you to settle down or be quiet when she needs to concentrate, your friend may be reluctant to ask you to be a polite passenger You need to take control of yourself, pay attention to what is going on around you, and be considerate of your friend who is driving.

❀ **Safety first.** Always buckle up; don't make your friend have to ask you. Keep the volume on your music to a reasonable level. Keep your arms, head, legs, and other body parts inside any moving vehicle.

❀ **The driver must have full control.** Do not attempt to hold the steering wheel, turn on the windshield wipers, shift, or put on the brake even if the driver asks you to. Those are his responsibility.

❀ **Don't abuse the driver's car privileges.** Don't ask or expect the driver to bend or break her rules. If she is expected home before dark, honor that expectation, and don't ask, tease, beg, or demand favors that violate her curfew or restrictions.

⊚ Offer to pay for gasoline. The offer to pay is not expected when you're on a date or if you're an infrequent rider, but if you ride often with your friend or depend on her for regular transportation, do offer to pay so she does not need to ask.

⊚ Don't litter inside the car or out. Clean up any messes. This can include offering to help pay for a trip through a car wash with a vacuuming included. Don't throw trash from the car or leave litter in someone else's car.

⊚ Be considerate of other drivers and pedestrians. Avoid yelling, whistling, and other behavior that can distract people and cause accidents.

THE GOOD SPORT

Good sportsmanship is knowing how to be a good loser and a good winner.

There are other equally critical components of good sportsmanship:

⊚ Following the rules—even if they seem "stupid"

⊚ Avoiding arguments with referees and judges (leaving discussions about calls to the captain or coach)

THERE IS NO I IN "TEAM"

Another way to think about sportsmanship: It's a collective win or a collective loss.

We win together; we lose together.

๏ Being considerate of other players

๏ Being respectful of coaches and their decisions

These same qualities hold true for the good sport in the stands who shows respect for the referees and coaches, does not bait the opposition, acknowledges good play (on either side), is considerate of those sitting nearby, and supports his team in a positive way.

There is a difference between loud cheering for your team and the angry screaming that comes out of the fan who has lost her temper. Back in 1945 Emily Post reminded her readers: "The quality which perhaps more than any other distinguishes true sportsmanship is absence of temper . . . not temper brought along and held in check, but temper

GOOD WINNING AND LOSING

Good Winning	Good Losing
Being happy but not boasting or gloating	Avoiding sulking, pouting, or complaining
Sharing appreciation for a good game with the loser	Congratulating the winner
Waiting until in the locker room or off the field for major celebration	Avoiding blaming others for loss: focusing on how to improve before the next game

securely locked and left at home." It was good advice then and is good advice now.

In high school the student who is the good sport is also likely to become a good leader. The game may be different, but goals are the same whether you are talking about a win on the field, a successful concert, or a championship at the spelling bee. And good leadership does not necessarily mean being the captain of the team or president of the student council. True leadership means serving as a model for others and influencing positive behavior through the good example of your own actions and attitudes. All your life you will have the opportunity to influence others. Who knows? That twelve-year-old in seventh grade you smiled at the other day may look forward to being just like you. What is the example you want to set? Once again the choice is yours. Now you not only are making a decision for yourself but, in a sense, are making a decision for those who follow. Consider it carefully.

A FINAL THOUGHT

Etiquette is all about thinking of those around you. How can you show someone respect? What is the considerate thing to do? How can you be honest without being hurtful? It's not always easy, but it's not really that hard either.

Picture this: Margaret works at Fred's Fries, the local fast-food place. Working at Fred's Fries is not easy. All day long she takes orders for hamburgers, cheeseburgers, fries, and drinks. The place is busy, and the line is always long. As you come through the line, you can say, *"Hi, Margaret, how's it going?"* and *"A burger and iced tea, please,"* and a simple *"Thank you."* Or you can say, *"Can't you just hurry up? This place is the worst."* What a difference a few words can make.

You have a choice. You can do something that may make Margaret's day a little better. You won't make a new friend. No one will pay you more. No one else may ever know. But Margaret will. And you will too.

So when you are choosing which manners you believe are important, remember the principles. Treat others with respect. Consider what effect your actions will have on those around you. Be honest in your dealings with your family, your friends, people you meet every day, and yourself. If you use these principles as the basis for your choices, you can be confident that the face you show the world is one you can be proud of.

INDEX